BUFFER THE BURNOUT

From Chaos to Calm
A Guide to Purposeful Living

NICOLE COOPER

First published by Ultimate World Publishing 2025
Copyright © 2025 Nicole Cooper

ISBN

Paperback: 978-1-923583-56-6
Ebook: 978-1-923583-57-3

Nicole Cooper has asserted her rights under the Copyright, Designs and Patents Act 1988 to be identified as the author of this work. The information in this book is based on the author's experiences and opinions. The publisher specifically disclaims responsibility for any adverse consequences which may result from use of the information contained herein. Permission to use information has been sought by the author. Any breaches will be rectified in further editions of the book.

All rights reserved. No part of this publication may be reproduced, stored in or introduced into a retrieval system, or transmitted in any form, or by any means (electronic, mechanical, photocopying, recording or otherwise) without the prior written permission of the author. Any person who does any unauthorised act in relation to this publication may be liable to criminal prosecution and civil claims for damages. Enquiries should be made through the publisher.

Cover design: Ultimate World Publishing
Layout and typesetting: Ultimate World Publishing
Editor: Anita Saunders
Cover Image Copyright: OszO-Shutterstock.com

Ultimate World Publishing
Diamond Creek,
Victoria Australia 3089
www.writeabook.com.au

DEDICATION

To little Nicole Simone Atkinson, you are safe.
And to my Uncle Alan, because you asked.

DISCLAIMER

This book is a work of nonfiction based on my personal experiences, memories and interpretations of events. While I have made every effort to present these events truthfully, they reflect my perspective and recollection, which may differ from how others remember them. For privacy and confidentiality, names, identifying details and events have been altered, combined or fictionalised. Any resemblance to actual persons, living or deceased, is unintentional and purely coincidental where not explicitly stated. The stories and opinions shared in this book are my own or that of clients and are not intended to malign, defame or harm any individual, group or entity. I have taken care to ensure the accuracy of all facts presented; however, this book should not be considered a definitive account or relied upon for legal, medical or professional advice.

CONTENTS

Dedication	iii
Disclaimer	v
Introduction	1
Part One: Why Am I Burned Out Now?	**5**
Chapter One: I Didn't See It Coming, or Did I?	7
Chapter Two: The Storm Raging Within	21
Part Two: Back to Basics	**35**
Chapter Three: You Are What You Eat	37
Chapter Four: Permission to Rest	49
Chapter Five: Dance Like No One Is Watching	63
Chapter Six: Rules That Become Fences	73
Chapter Seven: Discover the Artist Within	87

Part Three: Design a Life You Don't Need to Escape From   **95**

Chapter Eight: Who Are You Now?   97

Chapter Nine: Leverage the Mind   113

Chapter Ten: Ride the Waves   127

Chapter Eleven: Do Less, Live More   143

Chapter Twelve: Give Yourself a Break   163

Afterword   167

About the Author   171

Acknowledgements   175

Appendix   181

References   183

Want to Learn More?   187

Buffer the Burnout: A 12-Week Guided Reset for the Midlife Woman   191

Testimonials   195

INTRODUCTION

Overworking is the Black Plague of the 21st century
—Richie Norton.

My guess is you've picked up this book because you're feeling overwhelmed from constantly juggling the many hats you wear at work, at home and in your personal relationships? It's likely you feel frustrated or anxious about where your career is headed or what your life will be like as an empty nester. You might feel disconnected and unfulfilled despite being seen as productive and competent at work. Or you just feel something is missing but your brain fog keeps you stuck, unable to really put a finger on how you feel or what you need.

You're just drained and exhausted! On the brink of the fire in you burning out.

What if I told you it is possible for you to feel more connected to yourself and the people you care about, and to engage in joyous creative pursuits that light your fire, resulting in an overall lightness to your step that has you bouncing through your day?

It is possible, and my intention is this book will provide a launchpad for your recovery or prevention of the burnout syndrome.

Whilst burnout has been defined as a workplace syndrome with a set of predefined traits, this book is not designed to address those workplace issues. In my experience individuals who are suffering the type of exhaustion and cynicism that is symptomatic of burnout simply do not have the energy, confidence or will to address the organisational shortcomings. Instead, I provide information and action steps you can take to reclaim your personal power to improve your life. Once you feel renewed you may choose to lead the charge and address systemic issues in your workplace.

Each chapter provides an insight to some of the key experiences and learning that have shaped the recovery journey for some of the clients I coach and my personal experience. The last thing you need is a regimented, step-by-step, six-month strategy that will 'fix' you. What I do provide is bite-sized tools for you to build your buffers that fit your personal lifestyle. The tools are more than taking

INTRODUCTION

hot bubble baths (although I am fond of a magnesium soak so keep doing that if it feels right).

It is not necessary to work through the book sequentially. You can pick and choose what feels right for you. Try things on for size and ditch them if they don't feel right. I also provide more resources for the areas in which you may seek further information and to delve deeper into the topic at www.buffertheburnout.com.au.

Lastly, whilst burnout is not clinically diagnosed, I do recommend seeking professional advice from your trusted health practitioners if your symptoms persist.

Remember, your body is designed to do whatever it needs to keep you alive. You can learn how to listen to what it is telling you.

PART ONE

WHY AM I BURNED OUT NOW?

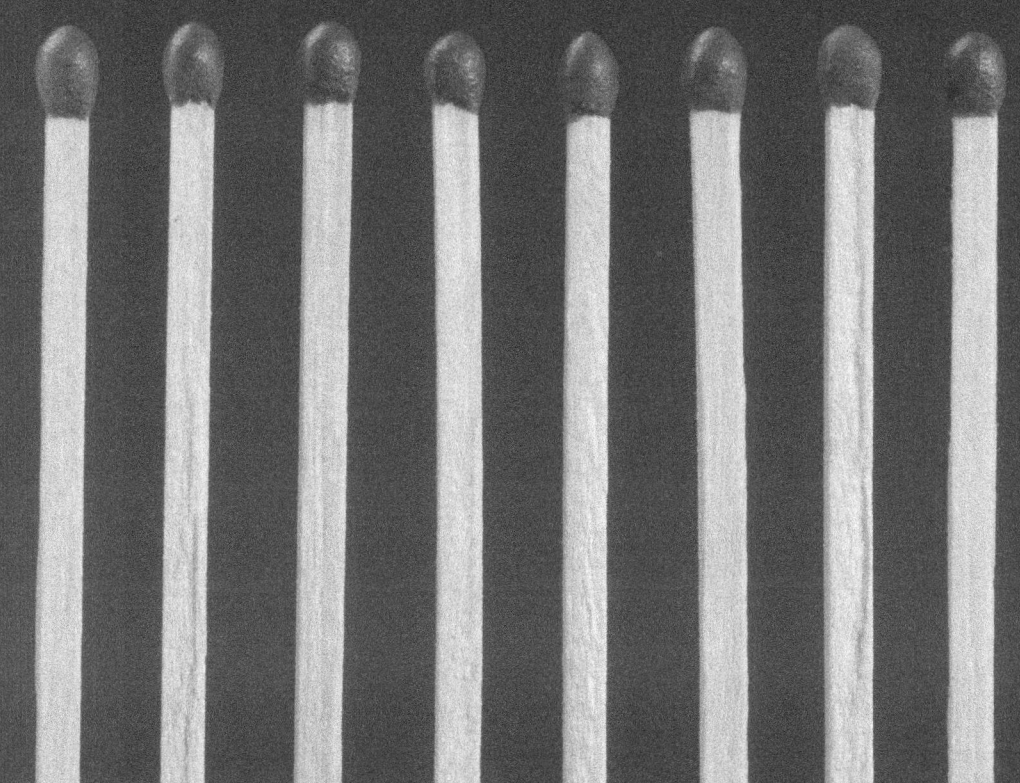

CHAPTER ONE

I DIDN'T SEE IT COMING, OR DID I?

You cannot burn out until you catch on fire
—Ralph Waldo Emerson.

It was a typical Saturday morning in May 2022 when I woke up, feeling an enormous sense of relief that the work week was finally over. My job as the business manager of a brand-new, busy secondary college was certainly stressful. The days were long, my responsibilities many and varied, and I was constantly flipping between tasks from early morning until late into the night.

Because we didn't have a full complement of staff, I took on multiple roles. Weekends were my relief and were spent one of two ways. I'd either take ages to switch off and spend the entire time on the couch, or swing straight into *Bugger it, work is not my life so I'm going to schedule the whole weekend doing all the relaxing things now.*

That particular morning, I dragged myself out of bed, pulled on my dressing gown and headed into the kitchen. Standing by the window, I flicked on the kettle for my ritual cup of tea and a slow start. As I stood there thinking about the schedule we had planned for the day, I felt a pain right in the middle of my chest. Not a dull ache, more like a sharp, stabbing pain right through the centre.

At first, I brushed it off. *Maybe I slept on my side too long and my ribs are stiff?* I tried to stretch it out while waiting for the kettle to boil, but nothing changed. The pain started to intensify. So, I did what any normal person would do.

I googled it.

The search results were alarming. *Go to the emergency department immediately.* Chest pain can be a sign for cardiac issues, and for women, the symptoms don't always match the classic signs, like pain down the arm, that we expect.

I scoffed. *Surely not me.*

I needed a second opinion.

I DIDN'T SEE IT COMING, OR DID I?

I messaged my daughter, a physiotherapist who works in a hospital, so she has some medical background. Her response was instant. *Get to the hospital now.*

After some humming and hawing, I finally told Geoff, my husband, very sheepishly what was going on. He decided to take me in. I went reluctantly.

This was just after the COVID lockdowns, when visitors weren't allowed in emergency. He dropped me at the entrance and went to wait at our son's place.

At the emergency department I was more worried about sitting around waiting for hours but as soon as I mentioned chest pain, I was taken straight through. No waiting room, no delays. Apparently, chest pain is considered a high-risk symptom.

That's when the frustration kicked in. I was mad at myself for being so ridiculous and wasting time. My time, Geoff's time and all the hospital staff resources.

My head was whining. *Why today? Why now?* It was a Saturday! I wasn't at work. We had plans to look at boats, to enjoy the day. I wasn't stressed.

And yet, here I was, hooked up to heart monitors, having blood tests every couple of hours, blood pressure and rate checks.

I didn't know it at the time, but this was a giant red flag that chronic burnout was taking its toll. My body was waving that flag frantically. It wasn't the only message it was sending either. For a long time, I just wasn't listening and paying attention to the signs of burnout.

What Is Burnout?

Burnout is not just a buzzword of the 21st century, but with no definitive medical diagnosis the term is used widely in the health and wellness industry to describe or diagnose various symptoms.

The World Health Organization (WHO) defines burnout as a 'syndrome conceptualized as resulting from chronic workplace stress that has not been successfully managed'. It is identified by three key characteristics:

Red flag one	Extreme and deep-seated exhaustion
Red flag two	Cynicism and detachment from work
Red flag three	Loss of drive, passion and performance

Currently the WHO definition states that it is explicitly in relation to the workplace and not in other areas of life, but the symptoms you feel spill into all parts of your existence. There is more conversation about whether burnout is only a symptom of stress in the workplace. Talk to any woman in her 30s or 40s and you'll hear the complexity of the stress they face as they juggle raising children, caring for ageing parents, all while balancing their physical and mental health as well as getting enough fibre, collagen, weight training and protein! Burnout symptoms don't go away when you're not at work or you are on vacation.

The physical signals of burnout are different for everyone, and your body may have been waving red flags at you for years. Common symptoms to watch out for are:

- Headaches or dizziness
- Disrupted sleep
- Body stiffness and joint aching
- Jaw clenching
- Getting sick often or not getting sick at all
- Loss of or increased appetite
- Repeated sighing
- Little or no energy
- Heart palpitations
- Digestion issues

What goes on in your head could also give you clues. Forgetting things or being easily overwhelmed by your to-do list. Even concentrating for long periods of time can be hard. If your inner critic becomes loud, constantly berating you for every small mistake, not being good enough or even constantly saying *What's the point,* there's a good chance that burnout is looming. This was another red flag for me.

Twice a week I attended leadership meetings with my strategy team. I was an active and valued participant.

Usually.

Looking back, I can see how burnout was taking hold. I stopped contributing and made myself small. I didn't speak up because I didn't have the energy to take on more work. And if I revealed that, I was scared they would find out I couldn't do my job as well as they could. I felt incompetent and ineffective. I felt alone.

When it came to solving problems, I had lost my care factor. On the inside I scoffed at new initiatives and in my head rolled my eyes (that *could* have been external too). When we had to address concerns that parents at the school were not receiving critical information my thoughts were *Are you kidding me? I'm working day and night!* When teaching staff expressed their frustration at being overworked and we needed to provide free coffee for their 'wellbeing' I let out a bitter laugh and a sarcastic *That will fix it.*

I had lost the will.

Burnout does not necessarily mean the workplace is toxic. Burnout can occur because of the type of work you perform, especially those industries that service people. Since COVID-19 there is more research going into these professions and many of the burnout studies have been in the medical and teaching fields.

Some of the increased factors that we experience in workplaces are things like the 'always-on' culture and society, with more readily available access to workers every day. Whether that be email or a multitude of ways of instant messaging, there are always people trying to get hold of you for immediate attention. When I started working in school administration in the early 2000s, it was unusual for colleagues to email each other for work tasks. What I have observed over time is that workers now are under the pump to produce more and it's quicker to email someone for a response or request than get up off your chair and have a conversation. It gets it off your desk and becomes someone else's problem. Productivity is expected to be much higher than it used to be. Long gone is the eight-hour workday, and people are working way more not to get the same work done, but to service more people.

The range of information that comes our way has expanded with notifications pinging to tell you that someone's paid you, or someone wants you to pay them, or indeed just to let you know that there's some great new thing on offer that will solve your exhaustion, weight gain or brain fog.

The characteristics of burnout are in some respects like symptoms of other mental health issues such as depression, anxiety and heightened responses to stress. Stress itself is not a medical or mental health diagnosis. Something happens, you respond, and it is our *response* to change or difficulty we experience that is the stress. We just use the term 'stress' as a short way of saying we're dealing with something big.

You may have increased stress because of another diagnosis. When we refer to being stressed, it is often a signal of how we are coping with difficult struggles in our life. Stress happens in our minds and bodies whether we are presenting a report for clients or colleagues at work, preparing for a birthday party or fixing a broken pipe that has flooded the kitchen. The level of stress we feel depends on what we think, feel or believe about the events, our abilities to complete the task and what we perceive are the likely outcomes.

The Cognitive Clutter and Gendered Roles Contributing to Burnout for Women

Women typically take on the role of nurturer, organiser, chief household executive officer, financial decision-maker, as well as the secondary income earner, or in many cases, the primary income earner. There are the obvious functions that happen in a relationship, family and home but there's a whole lot of other thinking, decisions and planning that is not so visible.

This is not a new phenomenon and has been talked about for many years. Emma (the French cartoonist) shone a light on the mental load women carry in her comic *You Should've Asked* in 2017 which provided a kick-start for more research and discussion about the increasing stress of remembering the little things, such as buying the nephew's birthday card, picking up dry cleaning or even watering the plants outside, or when to change the smoke alarm, vacuum behind the bookshelf or organise Grandma's birthday. These are the little things that add up onto the mental load for women.

Jenny, a full-time mum of two children under five and part-time administration assistant in a large primary school, felt this a lot. She told me during her burnout recovery that even though she had a supportive husband, Jack, he didn't seem to get it. One night she told him how she felt and asked for his help. Of course, he was obliging and was willing to take on some of the load. The sink had been blocking up for weeks so Jack announced he would get the plumber the next day. Relief washed over Jenny as she turned over to go to sleep. Until Jack asked, where do I get the plumber's number from?

Then we're bombarded with other messages of how we need to take care of ourselves so we can continue to be capable of doing everything, like 'Go and take a hot bath', and then women feel so guilty about doing this because they use all the hot water and then run through the endless to-do list, or the list of the things that they should have done but haven't, and then they feel like their nervous system is on high alert so they jump out of the bath to get moving and get it done.

Then you go to work because women can have it all. Somehow the feminist movement of the early 1900s that fought for equal rights, like voting, became the belief of many women that if you were truly feminist, you *had* to do it all. But is doing it all worth the price of failing health?

At work, you might feel that you're not recognised for all the effort you put in, or that you're the only one who is doing the work. Then, if you're not achieving and meeting deadlines, you feel like you're not enough. You're not doing enough, and on top of that, you're not even taking care of yourself. It means you're working harder but not getting anywhere.

What is missing is that sense of fulfilment, replaced by frustration, feeling like you're stuck and cannot change or pivot.

And amongst all this, a very lonely, deep-seated, isolated feeling, even when surrounded by others. Those connections somehow lost. Disconnection from family or friends, or even your passion and soul's desires: your dreams, emotions and ambitions are completely disconnected from your body.

For me, after my 'little' visit to the emergency department, I started worrying about death. I mean, I had just turned 50. How much longer did I have? There was still so much I wanted to do in my life.

Around the same time, I read a news article about a school leader who had died of a heart attack at her desk. Working on her own, working well past the end-of-day bell. The workplace took a proactive approach to health and safety with more discussion, surveys and initiatives about the growing stress for frontline school staff and then made changes to first aid equipment at school sites to provide for fast care in an emergency.

It's a great initiative, but it didn't really address the underlying issue, and that is, women are working harder and longer and are deeply stressed. In Australia, heart disease is the leading cause of death for women, with one in four deaths due to cardiovascular disease. High levels of stress for long periods of time is a factor that increases your risk of cardiac issues.

So, there I was at my desk, watching as the streetlights turned on yet again, trying to push through a report that was already overdue. Dismissing the ache that pounded my temples, the bubble that rose into my throat as I read another email demanding a response. As the tears welled in my eyes and I felt them spill out, I wondered, what happened to me? Why am I doing this? What if I died right here in my office alone? Away from my beloved husband and adult children, with grandchildren on the way. I didn't want this.

This was yet another moment that my body whispered something had to change. I started to look more into what my symptoms were telling me which has led me on a journey of discovery that continues to this day. The discovery of how the body, mind and soul can work together to buffer symptoms of chronic, long-term stress, and ultimately burnout.

Fast forward to the present day and I have reset my nervous system, rewired my brain and reclaimed my life. I sleep so well at night and wake up refreshed and happy to greet my day. I feel the full spectrum of emotions and know that my thoughts are critical to how I see the world and all that it throws my way.

So can you!

CHAPTER TWO

THE STORM RAGING WITHIN

Before we get into the buffers you need to know about hormones. Why are hormones important in buffering burnout? Well, as a woman in my 50s, those whispers, and sometimes they were shouts, in my mind and body at that time were very influenced by the hormonal storm of perimenopause.

Often when we're thinking about hormones, we think about those involved in controlling reproduction. Estrogen, progesterone, testosterone. Sound familiar? They're the specific group of hormones responsible for reproductive processes but pretty much every process in our body is influenced or driven by hormones.

Hormones are the chemical messengers released as a response from our endocrine system that affect many systems within the body. They have a role to play in whether you feel hungry or not, processes like cell production, the growth of muscles and tissues, metabolism rate, right down to the details of when to mobilise glucose in the bloodstream.

Some hormones are produced to stimulate other hormone production along the way. When hormones are released from a gland such as the thyroid or pituitary gland, they travel through the bloodstream until they reach the cell they are designed to stimulate. The hormone attaches to the cell via a receptor and performs the required stimulation needed. It's a bit like setting off a domino chain by knocking down one which in turn knocks down the next and the next.

When the body is optimal, producing hormones at the right levels to perform the right functions at the right times, the human body just feels on top of the world, and you feel that life is easy. When you've had a productive day and your hormones are working well, you go to sleep peacefully at night and wake up refreshed the next morning. It doesn't just happen because of your alarm. This is a response from the body that's regulated by the rise and fall of hormones commonly known as your circadian rhythm. When you want to wake up, enough cortisol is produced to energise your mind and to get your body moving and go about your day. When the sun goes down, cortisol production has reduced so the body starts to wind down and melatonin is produced to promote and regulate your sleep patterns.

There are many factors that can lead to our hormones becoming dysregulated. Some of these are just natural parts of our lives such as ageing which signals a change in how our hormones are produced. For women, we know that we go through hormonal changes cyclically, on average 28 days, and the demands for those hormones change over the course of our lifetime. Think adolescence, if a woman chooses to be pregnant, and the big one towards perimenopause and into menopause, when our sex hormones stop being produced because we no longer have eggs to ovulate.

Another big impact on hormone production is stress, and how we perceive the challenges in our life. I'm going to talk about the stress hormones and how they're linked to our sex hormones and what this means in burnout.

The Stress Hormones

Not all stress is bad for you, such as stress on the body itself. To build muscle you need to apply a load to the tissue, creating stress, to effectively break it and stimulate the growth of that tissue. Similarly, when you're in a life-threatening situation the stress response stimulates processes in your body to help keep you alive. You may have experienced moderate, short-term stress, say, when cooking a new recipe or learning a new move in yoga. That feeling that your head might explode as you learn new things or solve challenging problems is a stress response.

There are many hormones produced as a response to stress and the two common ones we often hear about are adrenaline and cortisol.

Adrenaline is a hormone that is released in an acute stress response. If you're in the wild plains of Africa and all of a sudden a lion starts chasing you, adrenaline would be released to mobilise the glucose in your legs so you could make a snap decision to either fight the lion or run to safety.

Most of you I assume are not in imminent danger of wild animals, but in the modern day, this could be equated to missing your morning alarm, running late for work, the dog has eaten your shoes, there's no food in the house and you get in your car only to find you need fuel. Then you hit a long line of traffic parked on the freeway and you are going to miss your meeting which potentially could lead to you being fired. Your perception of all these events can seem like a life-threatening episode that produces the same stress response and hormones in your body.

Your body is designed to keep you alive. The purpose of adrenaline is to make sure your body can do just that. It does this by reducing digestion processes, because in a life-threatening response, you need to fight or flee, and food isn't the priority. You will feel more alert; it heightens your awareness and increases your heart rate and blood pressure to prepare your body to get away.

For the body to use it effectively it is produced as an occasional response, because invariably we'd be going about our day without those threats of lions running through the streets where we live. But what happens over time is that when we are continually activating these stress responses, and adrenaline continues to be released, it can have long-term impacts on the body and the normal responses.

The hypothalamus is a part of your brain, and its job is to keep your body in balance and safe. It controls functions that you don't even need to think about like breathing and maintaining the right body temperature. It is always on, scanning for safety. This means safety both externally (are there threats coming towards me?), internally (have we eaten enough to get the energy we need?) and even emotionally (do they still like me?).

The hypothalamus works closely with the pituitary gland which is located in the brain just below the hypothalamus. The pituitary gland interprets messages from the hypothalamus to determine whether the body is safe or not safe. If it doesn't perceive safety, it sends a message in the form of a stimulating hormone to the adrenals and the thyroid. In response the adrenals produce the stress hormone cortisol to deal with excess adrenaline and sustained stress. During periods of chronic stress, say that lion chases you every day or your email inbox is at 800 unread messages every day, the body may be producing higher levels of cortisol.

Cortisol has several roles in the body including decreasing inflammation, regulating blood pressure, balancing glucose in your bloodstream and helping you get out of bed in the morning. Typically, you'll see a rise in cortisol upon waking, helping give you energy and vitality. Over the course of the day it reduces and by bedtime is lowest, ensuring, along with other hormones, you sleep.

High cortisol production can be a signal that the body is experiencing long-term threats and feels unsafe. During events like floods, fires and famine, the body would try to protect itself. In long-term stressful situations, the body is built to shut down any functions not required to stay alive. If the body senses there's no food, it will reduce your hunger and cease reproduction processes. No need to reproduce when there is no food. If fires or floods are raging, your body needs to be alert and awake to monitor the situation so you can keep safe.

More is not better. High levels of cortisol produced all the time results in negative effects such as interference with sleep, increasing fatigue, disruptions to memory and inflammation.

Contribution of Hormones to Burnout

Adrenaline is only designed to elevate occasionally and briefly. During chronic, longer periods of stress and continued high levels of adrenaline, stress and worry increase. The body wants to stay alive, so it sends a signal to increase cortisol to deal with the inflammation caused by constant adrenaline.

Cortisol is increased to slow that inflammation. But if symptoms or threats to safety don't change, the adrenals can't keep up. Either they can't produce enough cortisol to match the level of adrenaline, or they produce enough but the demand is too much, and it has no impact, like pouring water into a bucket with a hole halfway up the side.

The result can be severe fatigue, body aches and pains, weight gain and slower metabolism. This is commonly referred to as adrenal fatigue. This constant load on your body and mind can result in you feeling disconnected, drained and unable to cope. Enter burnout!

The Burnout Loop

While these stress hormones are being released, the production of sex hormones is also reduced. For women, when sex hormones are out of whack, it sends a lot of signals that something's not right. But society often conditions us to believe that symptoms like premenstrual syndrome, headaches, hot flashes or insomnia are simply 'normal' and that you can fix it with a pill, a heat pack or a hot bath. While they may be common for women, it is not necessarily normal.

But they are signals.

During times of tension, the production of stress hormones will always take priority over releasing sex hormones because survival is our most primitive instinct. In a crisis, reproduction is not a priority so less sex hormones are produced including estrogen and progesterone.

Estrogen's primary role is to prepare the female body for pregnancy. It also has an important role in good brain function, and it tempers the brain's stress response system. Hello, brain fog and anxiety buffer! Progesterone's primary role is to support a pregnancy and it's also an anti-anxiety and antidepressant hormone. So, when there's lots of stress and less progesterone, we become more sensitive, and more prone to symptoms of depression and low mood.

Women in their 40s and 50s at the end of their reproductive years often experience all of this at once. It becomes a vicious cycle. Low progesterone means increased anxiety and low mood. You feel overwhelmed. You start asking, *What's wrong with me? Am I just being a bitch?* That activates the sympathetic nervous system, which increases stress hormones, which lowers progesterone ... and on it goes.

That's one of the factors that gets you to that place of relentless exhaustion and burnout. When you ignore the role of hormones in the body, you get stuck in the chronic stress loop. Less sleep, more weight gain, feeling worse, more deadlines and your adrenals just don't know what's going on anymore. It runs deep, physically into your cells and emotionally to your core.

What Can You Do?

If you've spent a lot of time pushing through, always getting things done, there are simple tools to start shifting the responses in manageable ways.

We're conditioned to think that when you gain weight, as an example, you need to start a drastic new diet or a High Intensity Intermittent Training (HIIT) regime to get back to that magic number on the scale; however, this puts more stress on your adrenals. Your body now thinks you're in famine, or maybe you're moving hard and fast so it thinks that lion must be back, and more cortisol is released. The cycle continues. This is the opposite result that you are trying to achieve so let's start with the buffers that your body and brain will assess as safe and therefore, heal those symptoms.

Over the next chapters we'll look at remembering and developing core buffers in your body and mind. Right now, what I recommend is to just notice how you are breathing. Notice if your breaths are in through your nose or mouth. Where does the breath go to in your body? Is it filling your chest? Is it moving to your abdomen? Or are you holding your breath?

There are a lot of studies that shows how the breath and deep breathing practices, like in yoga or meditation, lowers cortisol. Deep, slow breathing sends a signal to your nervous system that you're safe. When you're not feeling safe, you breathe shallow and fast into the top of your chest. That signals you need to get away or fight which fuels your stress response and burnout loop.

Breath has a profound impact on your body. It mobilises oxygen through your blood and calms your heart rate, nervous system, your brain and your muscles.

BUILD YOUR BUFFERS

Try one of these breath practices.

1. **4-7-8 Breathing**
   Sit upright in a chair or lie down and get comfy.
   Close your eyes if that feels good or lower your gaze.
   Inhale through your nose and count for four seconds.
   Hold for a count of seven.
   Now exhale slowly for a count of eight.
   Repeat two to three times.

2. **Box Breathing**
   Sit upright in a chair or lie down and get comfy.
   Close your eyes if that feels good or lower your gaze.
   Breathe in slowly to a count of four. As you do, imagine beginning to draw a box with a line from the top left across to the right.
   Hold your breath for a count of four and draw that line down to the right corner.

Breathe out steadily to a count of four and imagine that line from the bottom right corner across to the bottom left corner.

Now before you breathe in just hold your breath for another count of four as you draw the line up the left side to the original start point.

Now proceed from step one for two to three rounds.

3. Alternate Nostril Breathing

Sit upright in a chair or lie down and get comfy. Close your eyes if that feels good or lower your gaze. You can use either hand for this technique and this is traditionally taught using your thumb and ring finger, but I sometimes use my thumb and forefinger.

Use your right thumb to gently press on your right nostril to close it.

Take a deep and slow breath only through your left nostril.

Now use your right ring finger to close your left nostril and at the same time release your thumb from your right nostril and breathe out slowly through your right nostril.

With the left nostril still closed, breathe in through your right nostril.

Use your thumb to close your right nostril and release the finger on your left then breathe out through the left nostril.

Start at step one and repeat as long as you feel called.

You can schedule time to do any of these practices throughout your day. Try one when you wake up; they are particularly useful at night to encourage sleep.

PART TWO

BACK TO BASICS

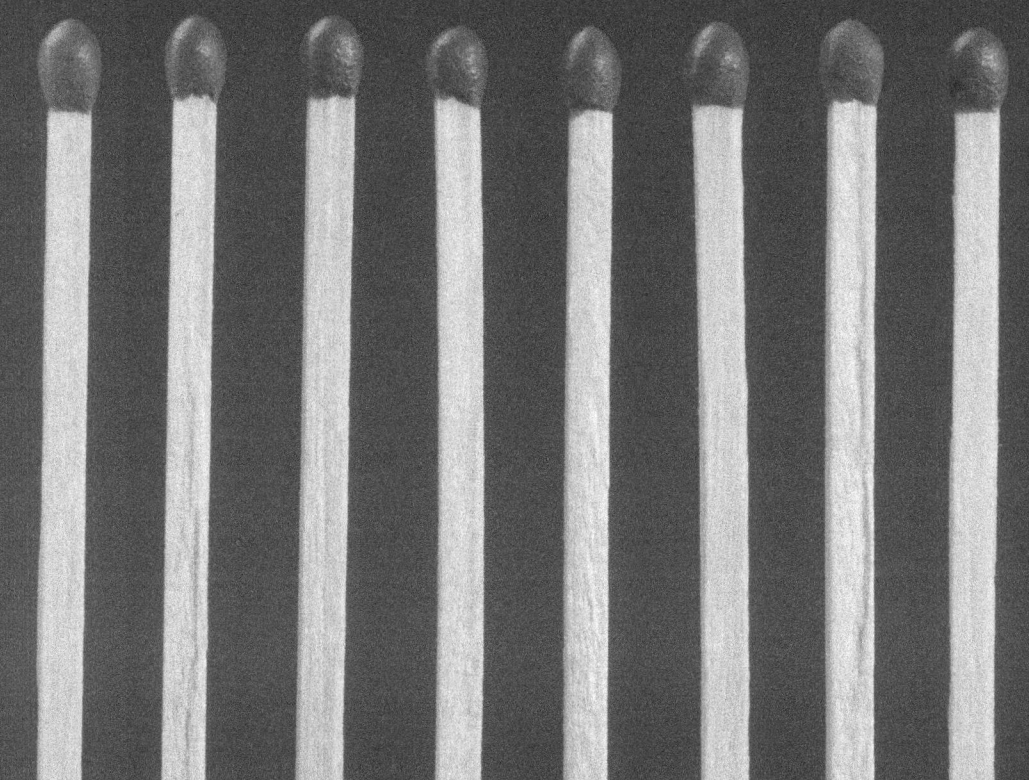

CHAPTER THREE

YOU ARE WHAT YOU EAT

You've no doubt heard the saying 'You are what you eat'. My grandmother used to say this over and over to me as I sucked the sweet, fairy floss flavours from yet another pink ridged musk stick when I was a kid.

You could write this off as an old wives' tale, but biologically, there is truth behind the phrase. Every meal is quite literally a transformation. Each single morsel of food, or other items, we ingest is in some form dismantled, reassembled and transformed into some part of you. It fuels trillions of biochemical processes with the intention to keep us functioning, healthy, recovering from illness or building muscle.

In simple terms, when we eat, our body breaks down the food starting with a very complex digestive system.

During digestion, macronutrients within those foods, like protein, carbohydrates and fats, are then broken down into smaller molecules to be used by the body for different purposes.

A simple example is that carbohydrates break down into molecules like glucose, which is absorbed into the bloodstream through our membrane walls. The absorption into the bloodstream provides an efficient transport system all the way through the body into the areas where it's needed. Remember the time you needed to run for the bus because you were late? Glucose is the fastest-acting fuel used to get your legs moving when you've activated the flight stress response!

There are other micronutrients and organic compounds, like amino and fatty acids, that when broken down into usable sources, go towards building cells or membranes essential for other functions to occur in the body. Phytochemicals, for example, are nutrients found in plants that play key roles in regulating blood pressure, decreasing bad cholesterol, preventing inflammatory responses or even protecting us against free radicals (unstable molecules) that cause cell damage resulting in disease.

It sounds simple, right? It *seems* simple but that's the magic of the body in its quest to keep the body stable and always balanced. Take the earlier example of using glucose as fuel. To make it usable, the hormone insulin is produced by the pancreas. Insulin's job is to help get the glucose from your blood and into the cells and muscles ready to be used as energy.

When we eat carbohydrates our blood glucose levels rise so more insulin is produced to stabilise sugar levels in our blood. Over time if we are consuming higher sugar foods for long periods of time our bodies can become less sensitive to the insulin signals which can result in what is commonly known as insulin resistance. This is where the pancreas can no longer keep up with the demand for insulin resulting in high blood sugar levels which is a risk factor for diseases such as type 2 diabetes.

Stress and the Insulin Resistance Cycle

In Chapter Two I spoke about the stress response and the role of cortisol. When your life is threatened or you perceive you are in danger, your body naturally produces cortisol which signals your body to release more glucose into the blood preparing you to fight or flee. This raises your blood sugar, even without eating anything, which is handy for your survival in the short term.

When you experience chronic stress over long periods of time, your blood sugar and insulin levels are constantly elevated. Add this to the insulin produced because you are relying on sugary foods to keep you going every day and your health begins to suffer. The symptoms of insulin resistance can include increased fatigue or energy crashes because glucose is not getting into the cells. This leads you to feeling more 'stressed' about not being able to cope with your day-to-day, so you rely on sugary or high-calorie foods to boost your energy. The cycle continues.

Food Is Not Just Fuel

Our choice of foods in modern day, for women particularly, is not just influenced by our body's need for nutrient-dense energy. It's often more complex than that and can be driven by our lifestyle, emotions, what we've grown up with and our environment.

Choices can be informed by what's convenient for our lifestyle. You're tired and need to get on to the most pressing demands of the day so grabbing a muesli bar to eat in the car saves you so much time in the morning. Timesaving, yes, but probably not a balanced meal providing the range of macro- and micronutrients your body needs.

Convenience can result in limited food choices. When we jam in as many tasks as possible in a day and we're faced with making hundreds of decisions, it can be overwhelming to think about how to include a variety of foods into our meals. We might rely on serving up the regular 'old faithfuls' to cut decision fatigue. We want food fast and dependable.

Food choices can also be linked to emotional memories and experiences even as early as our childhood. I recall as a child, whenever I was upset or injured, being offered something sweet and sugary like a lolly. It happened in many different circumstances: the nurse at school when she patched up my scraped knee; receiving good (or bad) feedback from a teacher on a test; comfort from my mum when my pet rabbit disappeared; a reward from my grandma for doing the dishes; and even a visit to the doctor resulted in a lollipop. In the brain these positive experiences trigger the release of dopamine, a 'feel good' neurotransmitter which is connected to the emotions we feel at the time. Over time, the brain associates sweet, sugary foods with comfort, love and soothing of emotions or pain.

Your nervous system wires together the experience of distress and the relief that comes from the sweet treat.

It works in the same way when food is seen as a reward. You might have grown up knowing that if you ate all your dinner and your greens, then you would have dessert. And if you didn't eat your greens or your dinner, you would not get dessert. Notice how this connection shows up as an adult. Go on a long hike, stop at a cafe for breakfast and coffee. Tell yourself 'I've been good all week, therefore I'm going to sit down and have a glass of wine at the end of the week to treat myself.'

Sometimes you're not sure exactly how you're feeling, but you find yourself standing at the fridge or the open pantry door, searching for something, but you can't quite decide on what to eat. It's not that you're hungry, or else you would make yourself a big salad and eat that nutrient-dense meal. You could be searching for the feelings in your fridge.

Sensory Triggers

Food is often driven by our senses.

Head to a movie theatre, and the first thing you smell is the hot, buttery popcorn, and you recall the times your grandmother took you to the movies as a treat. Years after your grandmother has passed, you yearn to have that closeness and connection so even though you're not hungry you choose the popcorn to reinforce those loving feelings of connection.

As sensory beings, it's not just about taste, but also the texture and the presentation of food, which can really influence how we feel about the food we eat. Watch a toddler eat and they will explore food by touching, looking and getting their hands (and face) right into it as much as they do by eating and tasting it.

Cultural and Social Aspects

Food is very connected to our cultural and social values.

For example, I live in Australia, and we have a very diverse cultural food identity, progressed by the many immigrants to the country.

Socially, it is a symbol of connection when everybody sits down together for a meal. You've heard the saying 'Break bread together', and this is one of the ways that we can connect with important people in our lives. The family barbecue on weekends is a prime example.

Nutrition and Stress Resilience

There is more and more research into the gut-brain axis and why what we eat is important in helping us build stress resilience.

The gut-brain axis is a two-way communication system between the central nervous system (the brain and spinal cord), the vagus nerve (the nerve that communicates between the brain and organs) and the enteric nervous system (a web of hundreds of nerve cells lining your gastrointestinal tract). In recent times, researchers have labelled the gut as the body's second brain because of the communication signals the gut sends to the main brain. Where we once understood that depression and anxiety may contribute to irritable bowel syndrome, bloating and stomach upsets, research now shows that these gastrointestinal issues can also send messages to the brain and influence mood. I experienced this first-hand every Monday morning for months. I would arrive at work and within hours have bloating, pain and cramping in my stomach which in turn contributed to increased brain fog and a general low mood for the rest of the day.

Vagal tone is a term used to describe how well the vagus nerve is functioning and currently can be measured by heart rate variability (HRV); that is, the time between each heartbeat. There is no standardised number that defines what good or poor vagal tone is and it is different for everyone. There are wearable devices that can track your HRV which can be useful to measure a baseline and track progress if you're looking to improve vagal tone.

Positive vagal tone improves many functions including digestion in our bodies. Similarly, having a healthy gut microbiome can have a positive effect on the vagal tone, ensuring that our bodies engage the parasympathetic nervous system (the rest and digest state) where we can effectively digest our food to mobilise the nutrients that we need for other repair and restoration processes. The act of eating on the run does not send the signals your body needs for digestion. Remember, running usually equates to danger so there's no way your digestion is required. Slowing down or moving away from your desk at work or the TV at home helps to signal mealtimes to your brain and body. Really noticing what you are eating, the colours, the textures and the smells. Chew your food! How often have you eaten a meal and forgotten to chew? Chewing starts the digestion process by signalling to your digestive systems that food is on the way.

The gut and the ability to move into the rest and digest state also affects hormone production. Microbes in the gut produce feel-good hormones like serotonin and dopamine which contribute to regulating mood and improving cognition. Some studies have shown that 90% of serotonin is produced in the gut. This is an essential part of combating stress and burnout recovery.

Practical Strategies

How do we use this to our advantage? Including lots of plant foods and a wide variety of meat, protein products and carbohydrates in our diets is essential to improve our body's ability to function and improve the gut microbiome.

It's also critical for us to practise somatic exercises (such as the breathing exercises in Chapter Two) to tone our vagal nervous system and be in that state of rest and digest when we're sitting down to eat. Somatic exercise is a type of movement and breath that connects the mind and the body with a focus on the internal perception and physical experience instead of external goals like increasing strength.

Just being mindful of how we eat and the type of fuel that we are taking on board helps, but this is not the time for fasting. The caloric deficit is only going to move our body back into a stress response.

Fasting can cause low blood sugar, which in turn activates a stress response. When the stress response is activated, further stress hormones of cortisol and adrenaline are mobilised, and in someone who's already in a state of burnout, this just exacerbates the chronic nature of the stress response and leads to worse fatigue.

These are all basic approaches, but they truly are effective for buffering the complex stress response in our body.

BUILD YOUR BUFFERS

1. **Eat a variety of plant food**
   Aim to eat 40 to 50 different plant foods each week. Keep a running list of each food you eat and record it once. So, if you eat salad every day, count lettuce on your first day only.

   Benefits include increased and varied micronutrients, increased and varied microbiome, and improved and stabilised blood sugar.

2. **Practise mindful eating**
   Designate a place with little screen distraction to eat meals. Chew slowly and engage your senses. It may help to describe your meal out loud. For example, I am about to eat my juicy grilled steak and colourful, crispy salad.

   Benefits include signalling safety for digestion and starting the digestion process. It increases the ability for your body to feel satisfied.

CHAPTER FOUR

PERMISSION TO REST

It takes courage to rest and play in a culture where exhaustion is seen as a status symbol—Brenè Brown.

It was thought for a very long time that during sleep, the body was completely shut down, and that shutdown was required, much like a computer, to rest and reset before the demands of the next day.

We now know that this is not entirely true. So many processes happen within the body and the brain during this essential part of our day. It's primarily the time when processes like repair, renew and regeneration of cells occurs.

It's a recovery tool that is required to improve our brain function, build essential processes in the body for muscle and bone growth, and repair essential physical areas as well. Perfect for providing buffers to day-to-day stress and preventing burnout.

Benefits of Sleep

There are many benefits of sleep and I'm just going to talk about some key processes that support burnout recovery, and why reduced access to quality sleep has the potential to worsen burnout symptoms.

Research on sleep has improved our understanding of the stages in sleep commonly known as REM (Rapid Eye Movement) sleep and non-REM sleep. Now what we know is that within non-REM sleep there are four different types of sleep which will help you understand how sleep happens for most humans.

The first stage of non-REM sleep is the window that happens between our being awake and falling asleep. As we move into being asleep, the second stage is where the body starts to slow down heart rate and breathing, and the temperature of the body drops. It's that blissful point where you feel your body relax and your eyes start to feel heavy and close.

From there, the body goes into a much deeper sleep for the third and fourth stages. These are the stages that are more important in the phases of sleep for actual consolidation of learning and organisation of memory, as well as being more restorative for your body.

After the non-REM sleep, you cycle into the REM sleep, and this is the one we know well, where the rapid eye movement happens behind our eyelids. Research has shown that during REM, the brain waves are like those of when we are awake, and this is sometimes where we end up in our dream state. It's at this point that the brain reorganises all the information it has been exposed to. The brain cannot keep hold of everything that it sees, hears, experiences or learns. It reorganises it into a structure that makes sense and can be easily recalled later.

We all know too that sometimes problems can be solved either during our dreams or as we're sleeping. You might be thinking over something that you've tried to solve during the day, and suddenly, you'll wake and have the answer because your brain has been able to connect thoughts and ideas and process the experiences. That's why it's quite important when learning new things that sleep is prioritised to consolidate the learning. This is the time when the neurons are firing and wiring together and at the same time, the brain can be discarding anything that's no longer needed.

Waking During the Night

Ever had that experience where you wake up every night of the week, or week after week, at the same time? It's always two or three o'clock in the morning.

In Chinese medicine, sleep disturbances between the times of 1 a.m. and 3 a.m. are thought to be linked to the liver processes. When you have recurring waking during that time, it can indicate an issue where the body is working hard to clear and transform what lands in the liver.

The liver itself is quite important in the body because it has a huge job to do in processing, not just the waste from our food and nutrients that we consume, but also the excess hormones that our endocrine system releases. It's where the hormones that are no longer required are broken down to prevent any further imbalance.

The liver, like many muscles and organs, requires glycogen released into the bloodstream to do this work. When you're faced with a lion that's going to eat you, your body is primarily focused on survival. It will release that stress hormone cortisol which increases glucose into the bloodstream to enable a rapid response of fight or flight.

But actually, you're just sitting in the office, and your body is now releasing cortisol and glucose to be able to deal with this all day. Because you're not running away from your email inbox, it's still roaming through your bloodstream ready for action. When your liver kicks in and perhaps it's trying to process any of the excess hormones in the bloodstream, it also requires glycogen to perform that function. Now the liver is working overtime because of all the extra waste it's having to deal with.

Hormones and Sleep Regulation

There are lots of hormones released which affect our sleep pattern. The biggest ones to know about are those involved in the regulation of sleep, and our own circadian rhythm or sleep cycle.

This cycle is influenced by a range of factors including light cues, and a hormone called melatonin. As the sun starts to set and night comes on, the body senses it's time for it to go into recovery phase, and so melatonin is produced. Melatonin has a soothing effect on the body.

Conversely, in the mornings, when the sun is rising and it is lighter around, that cues the body to release cortisol in order for us to wake up and feel refreshed.

The liver is responsible for helping to process any excess that is produced. That means melatonin wouldn't be continually released and circulating through the body, causing us to want to sleep all day, or cortisol wouldn't be continually released, keeping us awake during the night.

Falling Asleep and Mental Load

Most health professionals agree a typical requirement for an adult is about seven to eight hours of sleep for prime health.

You know it's important so as you prepare for sleep, you map backwards from tomorrow. *I've got to get up at 6 a.m., so therefore I need to go to bed at 10 p.m.*

You climb into bed at 10 p.m. and as you lie there you start running through the day's events:

- 'Did Jane really say that to me?'

- 'I can't believe that happened in the meeting.'

- 'I should have said that differently.'

Then you think of tomorrow

- 'I need to go to the shops to get a birthday present for Grandma.'

- 'I haven't been able to fix the tap in the kitchen that's still dripping.'

- 'Did I turn the dishwasher on? That reminds me, I'd better change the batteries in the smoke alarm.'

By now it's midnight and you've debriefed your day and created tomorrow's to-do list that seems a mile long. You look at the clock and start calculating how much sleep you are going to get now, pre-empting the alarm at 6 a.m. You roll over and best-case scenario you fall asleep by 1 a.m.

Now you are lucky to get five hours' sleep *if* you sleep soundly for the entire period.

What went wrong? Well, you started with the intention of going to bed at 10 which was exactly eight hours before your wake-up alarm. You've robbed yourself of critical sleep time. This approach ignores the process the body and mind need to wind down to enter the sleep cycle.

Improving Sleep

One of the big things that improved my sleep was thinking about the routines that I did once I wanted to go to sleep.

It wasn't simply just the calculation of eight hours: 'Therefore, 10 a.m. is bedtime because I get up at 6 a.m.'.

I needed to think about the wind-down ritual to allow my body to prepare for sleep.

I noticed that in our lounge room, despite having a dimming switch, I always wanted the lights on full. It would cause such a debate because others in my household wanted them low and I was always cranky about how I hated not being able to see when we sat down after dinner to watch TV. It was too dark!

One of the things we've talked about is how light affects and triggers the sleep hormones that help us go to sleep. Too much light stops that from coming. My brain literally thought it was still awake time.

I started to use the dimmer switch and turn it on low, pretty much from the time the sun went down. Similarly, I started turning off screen time, television, computers or even scrolling on the phone. I just needed to wind that up several hours before I went to bed.

Phone Habits and Night Routine

The next part of my routine was to remove my phone from the bedroom and plug it in the main living area. That way, the phone was then put away for the evening. Setting Focus on my iPhone for the sleep wind-down period was helpful as well because it muted the incessant pinging of notifications. You can always keep the notifications on for the kids and the people important and close to you but muting everything else significantly reduces the urgency of alerts.

Changing my evening routine by switching off the devices and screens meant I also switched to other activities that were much more soothing for my body. I rediscovered my love of reading. I don't read self-help books at night, that just gets my brain fired up with ideas and mental notes of things to try, but rather fiction that can activate the imagination.

Journalling and Somatic Practices

Another soothing task that you can add into the routine is journalling. I found this was useful. I would leave my journal on my study desk, which was on the way to my bedroom. Before I headed into my bedroom space, I'd sit and write for a few minutes, even if it was just notes on what my day was like.

Or it might be deeper, for example, a monthly prompt that I'm working on:

- 'How am I being creative this month?'

- 'What can I do tomorrow to be more creative?'

A word of caution. Do not use this time for planning in your diary and looking at what is happening tomorrow. You may be tempted to start pre-empting and thinking ahead to what you have to do and how you are going to do it. Or you might try to get ahead by 'just' checking your email which could go on for an hour or more.

If I knew I had to send an email, I'd be going to bed thinking, *I need to send that email. What am I going to say?* and literally starting to prompt myself like ChatGPT. Sure, I wholeheartedly agree with reviewing your calendar and email the day before, so you are prepared. Just schedule that task earlier in the day like just before or after dinner, or better still the last thing you do before you leave your workspace.

If journalling is not your thing, other useful practices like somatic exercises can help. For my evening ritual sometimes this would be practising yoga movements, and I would do these on the mat in my lounge room before heading off to bed. Other times, they could be done in my bed. Somatic exercises might include breathwork, eye movements or certain stretching activities, but low-key stuff that would engage and activate the parasympathetic nervous system into the rest and digest state.

Supplementation and Environment

Trying the practices can soothe the nervous system and help the process to get started. You might find that you need to consider your bedroom set-up.

Ensure you have a low light and that the temperature is a bit cooler. The ideal temperature for that rest and digest activation is much cooler than we normally think. Making sure that the room isn't too hot is important; an open window to get the cool breeze or having a fan on at night in summer could help.

Try not to use your bedroom for work and thinking tasks. Keep them out of the bedroom so your mind associates the space with rest. If you have trouble sleeping, a good tip is if you can't get back to sleep within 20 minutes, you get up and do something low-key, like reading in another room, then return to bed when you feel sleepy.

If you find yourself flipping the doona off and on during the night, consider making your bed in layers, ensuring you have some lighter layers depending on the time of year. If sleep is disturbed by restless legs or cramping muscles, consider seeking advice from a naturopath for supplementation. It is common for women in their 40s and 50s to experience these types of disturbances and can be related to the changes in hormones.

Final Thoughts

Improving sleep takes time. Our body's circadian rhythm and being able to reset it can be a long process. We do get into sleep habits, so patience and compassion with yourself while you're doing this process is important.

BUILD YOUR BUFFERS

1. **Create your wind-down ritual**
   Look at creating your sleep and wind-down ritual before bed and think about what your body, mind and environment needs.

2. **Use calming affirmations**
   As you settle into bed, try actively repeating phrases like 'I am safe. I'm tired. I allow my body to rest well'. You can access more affirming statements from my website.

3. **Journal daily reflections**
   Take a few minutes to write down three reflections about your day. It could be what you are grateful for, things that went well or something that made you smile.

4. **Track your sleep patterns**
   Try writing down your sleep patterns for a week to observe what your rhythms are and what disrupts them. For example, is it certain foods or activities that are happening during the week that you find are leaving you sleepless? Make changes based on your observations.

CHAPTER FIVE

DANCE LIKE NO ONE IS WATCHING

Movement for women over time has predominantly focused on what it does for our looks. If you were around in the 80s and 90s, you were subject to the exercise and fitness industry that advertised workouts aimed at sculpting the body or using it to create the calorie deficit to slim down faster.

I vividly recall a friend of mine, Moira, when we were in our early 30s who lived and breathed physical activity. Moira would get on a treadmill and run for two hours every day plus go to a one-hour exercise class five nights a week. I had lost my mojo with exercise at the time, so I asked more about her regime and how she was able to keep it up. She proudly proclaimed the only reason she did this was so that she could keep up with her love of drinking wine and eating chocolate while keeping her body weight stable! Sometimes, she admitted, she was on the treadmill *and* eating chocolate at the same time.

It wasn't unusual for women to have this belief in their head that they had to expend the same (if not more) number of calories in exercise as they consumed.

Calories in = Calories out.

The belief was further advertised and embodied by high-profile women who grew the fitness craze.

Movement is so much more than this.

The human, physical body is a masterpiece of evolution. Every muscle, bone and even cell is designed to keep you alive and our species evolving. For most of human history movement was critical for survival. As hunter-gatherers we needed to physically move to different places to source our food.

We needed to either fish, steadying ourselves in water, or even run after an animal to hunt. Similarly, we would have to squat and pick berries or reach up high for fruit hanging from a tree. If we were confronted by that lion chasing us, we needed to get up and run or perhaps climb a tree to escape.

Even as the agricultural era developed movement was still required to tend a farming lifestyle to prepare fields, harvest grains and prepare fresh produce for food.

When raising families, the body was designed to feed and protect our young, and as they grew, we needed to have the strength to lift them or carry them long journeys or during our workdays, strapped to our back or front.

Only in the very recent history of humans and the Industrial Revolution has our need for daily physical movement reduced. Humans developed machines to do the heavy lifting and increase production at the same time with much less effort on our part. It means less people are needed for food production so no longer is it the whole community's job to source food. The modern world provides convenient access to food without much effort. Some of us just need to get up and go to the shop to buy it packaged conveniently. Come to think of it, you can even get food delivered. Talk about preserving energy!

The body wants to move. Think about it, have you ever really been able to lie completely still? Even in sleep, you'll notice your partner will twitch and move, or you might have to shift your weight from left to right or move your leg in or out as you sit at your desk.

From a young age, we're developing and growing muscles, and movement has been shown to contribute to strengthening our muscles and helping our bones to grow and develop, critically important during those growth phases, especially through adolescence. As we age, without that movement and focus on strength, muscles start to break down. Use it or lose it! Keeping our muscles strong rather than losing them is important for the body to keep on moving the way it is intended well into our senior years.

Muscle grows when the body is challenged by moving against resistance or lifting weight. That process leads to the muscles breaking down—in essence, a damage or injury to the fibre of the muscle. The body's response is, okay, something is broken. Time to repair that damage. The body is adaptable and likes to make sure that it can go about the day in the most efficient way it can so the repair that happens within the fibres of the muscle then increases the mass or the size of the muscles to be able to lift that same weight without breaking again.

This doesn't just happen in isolation. There are a lot of other factors involved, like hormones and rest, that are required for the muscle to build, as well as particular foods and the inclusion of macronutrients like protein. What we do know is that building muscle requires a consistent approach and continually challenging the muscle with movement.

If you go to the gym lifting the same weight at the same time, your body adapts quickly to that, and you need to challenge it with increased load or effort to build muscle.

This is why your personal trainer will often increase the weights or repetitions on your workout plan to avoid a plateau in your results.

Other Benefits of Movement

Feel good
During and after physical movement, the body produces and releases endorphins, which are a form of amino acid that act as a messenger or neurotransmitter in the brain. Neurotransmitters bind to particular receptor cells in the brain for different reasons. In this case, endorphins bind to a receptor that triggers an increased feeling of pleasure and reduces the sense of pain. Ever heard of the term runner's high? It is because of this positive trigger in the opioid receptors that runners feel happiness and are more likely to *want* to go for another run. In fact, anything that you experience, either through pleasure or because your body wants to help you cope, can boost the release of endorphins. Beyond movement, studies show laughter, hugs with people or patting animals, meditation, listening to music or eating sweet foods provide the same positive responses. Addiction can develop by this same process and studies show that opioid drugs produce the same type of response.

In stressful situations, especially in chronic burnout, the release of endorphins can help to reduce anxiety for your brain and body to cope. Plus feeling good helps you enjoy your life.

Reduce brain fog
A study done at the University of British Columbia found that regular aerobic exercise can increase the number of brain cells, improve neural pathways and increase the size of the hippocampus, the part of the brain responsible for memories. This is beneficial for several reasons, including improved memory and learning. During times of stress, you can feel like your thoughts are scattered and many people describe the experience as brain fog. Exercise has been shown to reduce this feeling and strengthens our neural pathways.

When it comes to the body's ability to restore, we know that sleep is essential for restoration of lots of those bodily functions. Exercise has a positive impact on sleep quality, and mood. A study including resistance exercise and stretching showed both had a positive impact on sleep quality, and those in the stretching group were also shown to have improved reports of mood and reduction of tension and anxiety.

If exercise has all these benefits, you might think that more exercise would give us better benefits, like a greater ability to sleep and a reduction in the signs of burnout. Wrong!

Too much high-intensity exercise and not enough recovery time can result in a decline in female hormones that are needed, like estrogen or progesterone. That can also trigger a chronic elevation of cortisol. In turn, this results in increased fatigue, brain fog and other hormonal changes.

How Does Exercise Fit Into Burnout Recovery?

There is no doubt that movement provides many benefits in the prevention and recovery of burnout. And this can be challenging when you're feeling quite fatigued with no motivation or desire to get up and move. It can be really hard to start, but even small changes can have a great impact.

Kelly, a self-described workaholic who went above and beyond in her role as a manager of human resources, was recovering from burnout. The thought of going to the gym seemed like just another, enormous task to add to her to-do list. Instead, she just started small and had a simple goal to walk around the block, about eight minutes at a leisurely pace. Over time, as she started to feel good about moving, she progressed into adding in lunges up and down the driveway after the walk. That was it for the day. It was the entire goal achieved in the early days. Slowly Kelly increased the activity and fast forward a couple of years, she now walks 40 to 50 minutes six days a week, lifts weights a couple times, goes to a Pilates class once a week, and does Yin or somatic exercises most days of the week.

You may have heard the hype that high-intensity interval training (HIIT) is beneficial as we move from certain life stages, such as perimenopause into menopause. But honestly, you don't want to be doing this straight away when you're recovering from burnout. You don't have to go straight into a HIIT class or start an exercise program that's going to place more stress and anxiety on your body and brain. What your body is telling you is to find something that is fun, achievable and sustainable. Anything is worthwhile to get moving. It could be a dance or yoga class either in a studio or in your lounge room watching it online. Slow, gentle movements for you when you're recovering are important, especially if your movement patterns have been getting out of bed, to go to the car, to go to your desk, to go home and do it all again. Try five minutes of walking every two hours or when you finish a task during your workday. I had a colleague who used to go for a walk at lunchtime for 20 minutes to get lunch.

These are really easy movement 'snacks' to build momentum and keep active.

Over time, you'll be able to build your exercise tolerance levels after you start experiencing the benefits, like the improved mood and sleep, and just feeling good again.

BUILD YOUR BUFFERS

Movement snacks
- Try 10 squats while waiting for the kettle to boil in the morning.
- Switch on your favourite playlist and dance however you feel.
- Set your timer for five minutes and walk around your neighbourhood. When the timer goes off turn around and go back.
- Look for Yin Yoga classes on YouTube and try one out on the weekend. This is soothing for your nervous system (more on this in Chapter Ten) as well as providing movement.
- Keep your water bottle in the kitchen rather than on your desk. Set a timer for every 40 minutes so you have to get up and get a drink. Chances are you need a toilet break too.

In fact, I do, so I'll see you in the next chapter.

CHAPTER SIX

RULES THAT BECOME FENCES

Give up the delusion that burnout is the inevitable cost of success—Ariana Huffington.

When I was in high school, I remember the tasks that were assigned in English classes would have a timeline mapped out. As an example, if the book report was due in four weeks, the outline would have a breakdown of the tasks required. Week one, do a brainstorm; week two, write a draft; week three, edit the draft; week four, submit your final copy.

I often found myself going from brainstorm, skipping the whole draft process, and creating the final piece. Then I would get an okay grade with comments like, 'Could do better with more refinement'. I found that I would tell myself I had done a terrible job due to not having enough time when really, I had not followed the process allowing myself time to produce drafts and edits as suggested. I didn't change much as I grew older, and it showed up in many different areas of my life. I had a belief that whatever I did, I had to be good at it and get it right from the get-go.

Now, don't get me wrong. I'm good at a lot of things. But what it did mean was that it took a lot of effort for me to maintain and achieve that level of expertise at everything I did. Sometimes this was at the expense of my own wellbeing and the type of relationships I wanted.

When I was raising kids, I read all the parenting books and decided that everything had to be just right for me to be the perfect mother. I had to have all their food made from scratch so they would be nourished well and their clothing made from scratch so they looked good. They had to be doing certain activities at certain ages to ensure their growth and development was right on time.

I even noticed this in my own self-care practices. In yoga classes, I found I was striving to take my stretch further than I could the day before because more is better, right? I was always trying to improve on it.

The same thing happened when going for a walk. I couldn't simply just walk at a leisurely pace to enjoy the scenery. It was always a hustle to elevate my heart rate because I needed to lose weight or get fit, or I just needed to get where I needed to be on time. I worked at such a high intensity all the time and I was always trying to improve my capacity no matter what I was doing.

And honestly, this served me well for a time. When I had one job to focus on, say, as a student, I could manage it. It took enormous effort, but I did it. Looking back though, it was much harder as I aged and my roles, interests and life expanded. I was trying to keep a house, family and job, then I had other interests, hobbies and volunteering, not forgetting self-care which involved balancing calories in and calories out. Trying to have everything just right and be perfect, and be the best at what I was doing, became utterly exhausting as I juggled all those balls at once.

Fast forward to my dream job as a business manager and building a new school. With less staff and resources, I was juggling everything from budget control to putting out chairs for parent meetings, and at that same time I was moving through perimenopause, had adult children getting married, a family member was dealing with cancer, my brother-in-law died, we were doing major home renovations and of course, this was during the time of the COVID-19 pandemic. All this pressure and stress became the catalyst for me to question what it was driving me because my body started to stop working as I *thought* it should and my brain was so full with so many tabs open that I could not see my way out. It was like all those balls I was juggling were now on fire!

Something had to change.

I started reflecting on how my beliefs of perfection were created starting from childhood. One memory was coming home with a spelling test, and I got eight out of 10. I mean, really, 80%! What a terrific achievement. My very well-meaning parents, who just wanted me to be amazing and the best that I could be, responded with, 'Good job. But what happened to the other two? What are you going to do next? What can you change for next time?' Like most humans, I just wanted to please my parents and live up to their expectations. And so, I created these standards in my head that for every achievement, I needed to strive to be even better.

Everything I did meant that I had to work extremely hard to be better than the last time. This push and drive didn't come just from my parents. My school reports and teachers reflected similar comments. The driving test. My boss debriefing me on customer services as a teenage restaurant server. The list went on.

Enter the perfectionist people-pleaser.

People-pleasing is not just used to describe people who are always easy-going or agreeable. It is a term to describe how people behave to gain the love and affection, acceptance or approval of other people. This behaviour is a fundamental, primal human need as being part of the group or tribe improves our chances of survival.

Behaviours are created starting in childhood and are influenced by the environment that you work and live in. The behaviours aren't always negative. In a primitive way, sharing food and displaying generosity can send messages to other humans that you can be relied upon in an emergency like a famine. In your family group or community, others will want to keep you close by as an asset to their survival toolkit.

The kicker is when you make all your decisions and behaviours based on the praise you receive from others, seeing this as a definition of your self-worth. Your identity becomes focused on the idea that serving others is more of a priority than serving yourself.

For me, I was juggling so many balls. Not only did I want to be the best at everything that I could do, but I also wanted to do everything to fit in all of the wonderful interests in my life. I wanted to be seen as helpful to others and look good while doing it. I wanted to feel accepted when others saw me so they would like me.

I received all the validation I needed to reinforce the belief that my self-worth was defined by my ability to do all the things for others. People would say to me all the time, 'How do you do this? You've got four kids, and you work, and you volunteer and sew your own clothes' and 'You're so good at *everything*'. My body and brain received the message I was doing life right!

There I was, producing amazing results in so many areas of my life, but of course something had to give. The sacrifices that I made were things I could control myself that weren't obvious to most people at first. I sacrificed sleep. I worked more time in the day than I didn't. I didn't spend as much quality time with my family, or my food planning, or eating, or movement, and resting was simply out of the question (mostly because my body was always on high alert ready to do the next thing). The list could go on.

Now I thought there was no end to my capacity and if I couldn't do and be it all, I was not doing enough and needed to do better. Science proved me wrong and the universal laws demonstrate the breaking points. There are physical constraints in time and energy. You can only be in one place at one time. Even the speed of light has a measurable limit and is not infinitely fast. I was brought up thinking multitasking was a highly developed skill. What science shows us is your brain is not completing multiple tasks efficiently at the same time. You're just task switching which means that completion is slower, and accuracy is reduced compared with focusing on one task at a time.

Your brain has a limited working memory, and your attention is a finite resource.

Even my grandmother would make that clicking sound with her tongue and tsk tsk at me to say, 'You can do anything but not everything all at once.' She didn't know the science but maybe the woo-woo of universal laws to demonstrate this concept. The law of cause and effect says, 'Every action has a consequence.' So, after all the hustle comes a big stop. The law of correspondence, 'As above so below', suggests that patterns repeat across different scales and your inner world reflects your outer world. My head was overfull and busting at the seams. At the same time, I had a pile of filing in my office that overflowed its container, and at home my wardrobe was cluttered and unorganised.

Enter the High-Achieving, Perfectionist People-Pleaser

Overachievers and high-performance individuals are more likely to burn out, simply because they work super hard. Then comes the fear of never being enough.

Perfectionists who constantly strive to be better are always focused on the next level. On the outside, this can look like they rarely celebrate or acknowledge achievements. Internally, not accepting those achievements. Others might be saying, 'Wow. That's such a good job.' But on the inside, the perfectionist people-pleaser might say thanks, yet will be listing all the mistakes and the ways it should be better next time. They will continually strive to do the next thing. For a long time, despite Leadership Award nominations, winning the best job in public education, starting a school from scratch, developing teams and processes, I really struggled to actually acknowledge my wins or achievements, big and small.

The Circuit Breakers

Letting go of the expectations of the high standards on oneself can really improve things, but it takes practice. A lot of practice. Your body and brain have functions to keep you operating in the most efficient, stable way. Making a change takes too much energy and your body will try to do what it knows.

When the belief that productivity and achieving is a statement of your self-worth, the brain will prove you right. The Reticular Activating System (RAS) keeps this belief forefront of the mind by noticing when this is true. Whenever somebody is praised for doing a good job, achieving really high, or 'look at how much they're doing', the brain looks for evidence to reinforce that belief. This perpetuates the harmful cycle of achievement equals self-worth. That can also bring in another harmful cycle of beliefs about rest. If the high achiever takes rest, this goes against what they know resulting in shame and guilt.

RULES THAT BECOME FENCES

You can use the RAS to your advantage to buffer the burnout or during recovery and times of stress. You're likely very familiar with setting lofty goals for yourself. We're going to interrupt that pattern and shift the goal post to a more achievable place.

The goal is to celebrate your wins. Not the big goals that take 26 steps to reach. Focus on the small things that make a difference to how you feel. Each day or week, record your wins. Here's a sample of real-life examples from me and clients I coach.

- I ate breakfast before noon, not at 3 p.m.
- I played music on Saturday while I cleaned the house.
- I enjoyed cuddles with my husband.
- I left work on time.
- I walked the dog each morning.
- I prepared a nourishing lunch three times this week.
- I went to bed before 10 p.m.

At the end of the week, read over your wins and feel good about yourself for a job well done. Over time, you can become better at accepting the praise from others because you've practised it yourself.

No More, No Less

Good is enough.
Done is enough.
Enough is enough.

As a perfectionist and people-pleaser, as an overachiever, you might find yourself rushing to the final product, the destination, without all the messy in-between. This is an easy trap to fall into because of the dopamine hit you get at the end when you achieve the results plus the effect it has on your brain. Again, practice is key here.

I wanted to let go of the perfection of getting it right first time, so I started to map out projects with smaller tasks and assign chunks of time to them. For example, I love to sew my own clothes. I'm currently sewing a skirt, which I need to take on a trip. Over two weeks, I mapped out the total amount of time I would need to spend to complete the task. Then I broke down the project into smaller sessions of between two to three steps to complete on most days. I did no more and no less of what I planned.

It works the same with any project. If you have 27 tasks that make up a project you can schedule just two steps each day to complete. Or you can set a timer for 20 to 30 minutes. That way, you get used to smaller contributions building to the outcome. No more. No less.

The Boundary of No

Have you ever had that invitation to attend an event, and you really don't want to go? Your friend begs you, 'Oh please, just go with me. I don't want to go alone!' It's not your cup of tea. You go anyway, and then you feel resentful about it because it takes you away from whatever else you wanted to do. Or maybe the event just doesn't align with your values. The resentment grows and you feel like you never have time for yourself, so you turn the shame and guilt critic inward. Why can't you just say no? It is hard to say no to people, especially when we are invested in the relationship.

- Start with low-risk or low-stake tasks where you can simply decline. Anything that was a courtesy invitation, decline.
- Give yourself some space, maybe 24 or 48 hours, by providing a response like 'Thanks, I'll get back to you.' In that time, you might be able to craft a respectful way to say no.
- Come up with clear ways of saying no. If it's not a 'Heck, yeah', it's a no. It may take a while to know what a 'Heck, yeah' or a 'Heck, no' feels like for you.
- Know that saying no is enough. You can say 'Thank you for thinking of me or your invitation. I'm not able to commit to that at this time, but if something changes, I'll let you know.'

You are enough to just say no. You don't have to explain with 10 reasons why something is no good for you. You can simply say no, thank you.

You don't have to apologise for not doing something for someone else. People will respect you for it. There's nothing worse than committing to things you don't want to do or can't do. Giving a clear answer helps you both know where you stand.

BUILD YOUR BUFFERS

1. **Ask for edits**
   At work, produce a draft document and submit it for feedback from your colleagues. Write a poem, short story or an article and ask for feedback from a trusted friend or family member.

2. **List your tiny triumphs**
   Look for the small wins and record them. Sometimes you can't see the wood for the trees but having a list can remind you and engages the RAS to seek out more.

3. **Build a boundary**
   Say no at least once this week. Find the low-risk place you can start to say no.

CHAPTER SEVEN

DISCOVER THE ARTIST WITHIN

Creativity has been shown in research to combat the effects of stress, and in turn, being more creative helps to expand the imagination.

Most people refer to imagination and creativity to mean the same thing. Imagination is really when we picture things, so visualising in your mind what something could look like. It doesn't necessarily have to be something that's already tangible. It might be a different way of thinking of something. If I say to you, imagine a gorilla on a red ball beside the lake. It's not a scene you've likely seen before but you know what the individual images (gorilla, red ball, lake) look like so your imagination can do the rest and put them together. Now if I say imagine a teacup, each person will come up with a different image and some may even see a picture of a cup shape that we've never seen before.

Creativity, on the other hand, is the active pursuit of turning ideas in your head into tangible stuff, physical things. That's where you either build on something existing or make something entirely new. Take the cup vision. Maybe you imagine a traditional teacup but added a spout to make drinking easier for someone who can't purse their lips. You could set about using some materials, maybe clay, to form the shapes together and voilà! You've created what your mind imagined.

Some of the ways to improve your imagination is by taking part in active creative pursuits. Activities like reading, particularly in the fiction genres, or visualisation, or taking part in artistic hobbies have been shown to improve the neural pathways that happen in your brain to connect to a more imaginative process. It also improves cognitive function and releases dopamine giving you more of that feel-good response.

Another way creativity significantly helps reduce stress is reducing levels of cortisol during creative art-making processes. A study showed that cortisol would significantly decrease after about 45 minutes of creative artmaking. It's helpful, particularly when you're stuck in the constant overthinking and chronic stress.

What creative art does is take you away from overthinking, when you can just enjoy the process of putting paint on a page without overthinking what it is you're doing.

Similarly, some people really find doodling beneficial. If you remember back in high school when you were bored in economics, you sat in the back of the room and just doodled, drew pictures, abstract or representational icons.

There are other ways that you can explore creativity. Journalling is another way that you can get your creative juices flowing. There's a technique that's called freestyle journalling, or stream-of-consciousness writing, where you can either start writing whatever's coming out, or use some prompts and see where it goes. Don't think too much about structuring it. You just put the words on the paper, and it's a useful way of telling a story and experiencing how that feels when you express yourself through that story.

Now I know that this can seem daunting at first. If you're like most people, you feel like you can't … you're not creative or the artistic type. Whose voice is that? Did you hear somewhere that left-brained people are logical and only right-brained people are artistic? Whilst it's true that the right and left hemispheres do have specific functions, both sides work together and the myth that people are more dominant in one side has been disproven. Anyway, I'm not expecting you to be the next Michelangelo (although maybe you are!). That is not the intention. The idea is to practise and explore your creativity, however that looks.

An internet search for art classes will bring up a range of different options. Look for something that's guided and time-specific, like two or three hours. There's a lot of classes that offer painting and drinks alongside it. Grab a friend or go alone and connect with new people.

I even recently did a very quick one. It was 45 minutes, finger painting in the dark using neon paints. It was held at an observatory here in Perth, and we were able to look through the telescopes at the moon and the stars. Did my painting turn out the best? No, not really. Well, it's still good in my grandkids' eyes, but it wasn't the purpose of the class. It was the connection to art. Really, there was no time for thinking. Just paint on a page.

There really are lots of quick and easy ways to explore this. Perhaps reading is more your bag. You might just start exploring some fiction. Losing yourself in those stories helps to down-regulate your nervous system, and you start to create those neural pathways. As you're reading those stories, you're forming the images in your own head, not necessarily how the author intended it, but the way you are interpreting the words and the story, and the narrative is yours and yours alone. It's a powerful way of reconnecting with your creative imagination. Even if full books are too daunting for you, look for short fiction stories for bite-sized reads.

The creative arts and unlocking your imagination helps to down-regulate the nervous system and put you into the parasympathetic state of calm and connectedness. It moves you from fight, flight or freeze into rest and provides benefits for putting buffers between you and chronic stress and burnout.

BUILD YOUR BUFFERS

1. Make something with your hands
Find an art class to explore creativity. Look for something that interests you from painting, drawing, clay pot making or anything else using your hands.

2. Write something down on paper
Try stream-of-consciousness writing. Set aside some time to write just three pages on paper. Let anything and everything come out and be written on the page.

3. Read something new
Visit your local library and choose one of the fiction books on display. Libraries usually have weekly or monthly highlights with new releases or a focus on topics of interest. We're going for something to stimulate your imagination, not another self-help book.

PART THREE

DESIGN A LIFE YOU DON'T NEED TO ESCAPE FROM

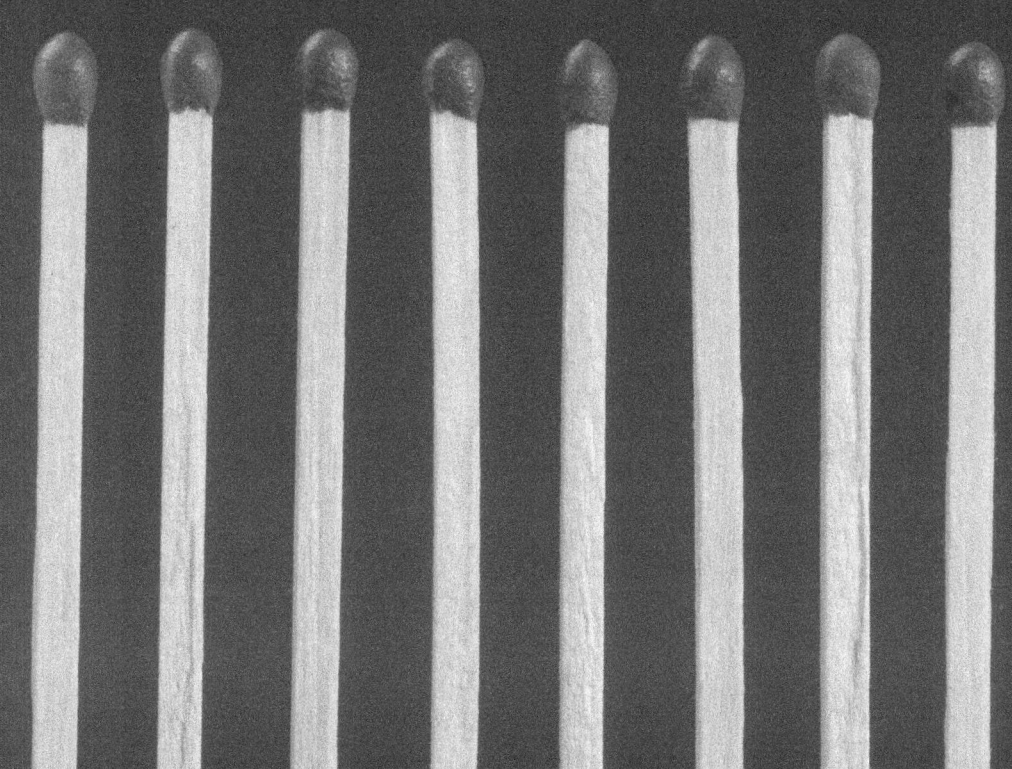

CHAPTER EIGHT

WHO ARE YOU NOW?

Burnout is what happens when you try to avoid being human for too long. Reconnecting with your values is how you return to yourself
—Emily Nagoski and Amelia Nagoski.

When you are experiencing burnout and trying to decide what to do next, it's possible that you feel like you are moving through molasses that's thick and sticky. Resisting even the smallest moves. When you look up you are surrounded by a thick fog and can't even see your way out.

What if you lived your life on purpose and made a difference every day? How would you feel? Could you see yourself moving through your life feeling clear and fulfilled, feeling like you made a difference, feeling like things could just work out? One way to experience this is by living aligned with your values.

What are values? How do we know that we're living aligned to what we value? Some people might use value words to describe themselves but it's more than words. It's what we do most days that demonstrates our values. Simply, values are the principles we live our lives by. They're made up of lots of different beliefs that we have formed over time. They can be influenced by morals and ethics, either from our parents or significant caregivers, or the environment and culture that we live in. Those beliefs can also turn into the standards that we create to live our lives by. From simple standards, like how I make my bed each morning before leaving the house, to more complex standards like how I expect to communicate with my significant other and people at work.

Our values are the things we do every day. They're the things that inspire you, give you energy and passion. What are the things that you like to talk about? Where do you find the awe in your life?

A simple way to look at what you currently value is by having a look at your bank account. In your mind, you might say, *I value health*, but when you look at your bank account and see transaction after transaction for fast food delivery or television subscriptions, are you valuing health? Or maybe it's convenience that is more aligned with what's important to you? Remember, nothing is right or wrong about this. Life is a continual journey with ebbs and flows. Periods of your life will look different than others and will look different from other people.

How Values Are Formed

Our values start to be formed when we are babies and young children. Along with our natural instinct for survival we want to avoid pain and move towards pleasure. As children grow and learn, parents provide the guidance and project their own values onto children. For example, fish and chips on Fridays could be a demonstration of a Christian value or ideal. This influence starts with a child's mother and father and then builds as children connect to other significant adults such as grandparents and teachers as they start school.

In adolescence and adulthood, the circle of influence becomes wider within the community and indeed the world, and we start testing our own independence and trying different perspectives to see what values fit. This phase can typically last right through until midlife which often becomes the point the typical 'midlife crisis' can occur when we start reflecting on whether these values are ours or somebody else's.

As adults, over 90% of people unconsciously live by someone else's or society's perceived values. This is mostly demonstrated when we have thoughts such as *This is what I 'should do' or what I 'must do'*. It is normal for you to want to fit in and conform to the values of the significant people in your life as it gives you a sense of belonging and acceptance. Belonging is an essential need for our survival and over time humans have evolved ways to ensure we stay connected to the group to stay alive. Hunting for food and defending predators was easier and more successful in groups so having the same thoughts, values and beliefs as those around you made this so much more efficient.

Benefits of Using and Living With Your Values

Not only do they provide fulfilment, but values also connect you with your identity. This means that when you're living truly aligned with your values you feel authentic. Living in alignment with values also helps you appreciate the relationships and values that others have because you know how important it is to them.

One of the ways I explored my values was reflecting on a story from my work. When we were growing the school and starting out, often the day was filled with back-to-back appointments. I prided myself on having the ability to transition easily through this phase by using a concept called the Third Space.

The Third Space is a technique to provide a mindful transition and is mostly applied to the transitions between work (First Space) and home (Second Space). It takes three steps. Reflect firstly on the context you were in and close any open loops. Step two is to rest. This can be a simple breath, mindfulness or grounding activity to bring you back into the moment. And lastly reset and prepare for how you need to show up for the next meeting. Is it empathy and compassion needed for your meeting or is it crystal and sharp focus to balance the budget?

Sometimes it felt like I was asking 'What the hell just happened?' and 'What is next?' Now, I was great at this. I was able to switch my attention between all the contexts I needed ensuring I was focused on the next thing or person without the last one influencing my behaviour. It meant I could come out of a meeting where someone was emotionally charged and exasperated, then go into the next meeting with a fresh perspective and not pass that energy on into that space.

Like I said, I was exceptional at this and practised it every day. I had so much practice because we worked non-stop from dawn till dusk, moving from one thing to the next.

I could go from home, dealing with my early adult daughters arguing over the hairdryer and bathroom time, straight to work where I was liaising with builders about complex construction issues. On to a meeting about marketing and developing the website followed by working with parents about enrolling and feeling worried about their child with a disabilty, before sitting at my desk balancing a multi-million-dollar budget with finesse.

This ability meant that those relationships were developed and supported, I could be relied upon and the meetings and the work got done, but over time, this became more of a hindrance. The 'Third Space' became more of a deficit for me because, what I did not realise at the time, it was starting to have a cumulative effect of eroding my ability to think, strategise, problem-solve and put things in place. There was no space in my day to do that because I simply moved from one transition to the next. I used the tool to get more done and be more productive instead of practising it to focus my presence.

And while those interactions felt good for those people or the work I was doing, it wasn't feeling good for me. Creativity and freedom are core values for me, and I needed space to express that in my work. The relentless pace of activity, coupled with the ability for me to keep fitting more in my day, was slowly eroding my satisfaction and connection to myself and meaning in my work. Now I didn't know this when I was in the thick of it. I just knew that something felt off.

When I first came across the concept that living misaligned with my values might be a key factor in burnout, I was asked to list what my values were. At the time, I simply couldn't articulate anything. I just didn't know where to start.

I'd always thought that family was high on my values list. I had four kids, for goodness' sake—I must have liked them! The reality was, I wasn't spending the time at home with my family. I was so invested in my work, and that took up all my cognitive, physical and emotional attention. I felt really confused.

Interestingly, when I sat down to think about issues or topics or activities that would light me up, I also found that hard. My mind was just blank. However, when it came to talking about the activities that *didn't* light me up, things that frustrated me, that list tumbled out onto the page like I'd tipped a bag of marbles onto the table! I listed all the things I was currently doing. It wasn't a good sign and just showed that I really was not living and behaving aligned with what was truly important to me.

Then I started to question, *how on earth did I get here?* I began to think about what I wanted my life to look like. I had to start assessing what areas in life were doing okay and what areas were not so satisfying. I could use tools like prioritising the areas in my life most in need, and identity was one of them.

Identity and Purpose

Your values act like a compass that shape your behaviours and decisions and what you will be known for. For example, if you highly value innovation then you would be known as someone who asks lots of questions and tries new things.

Your identity is what you tell yourself about who you are. This comes from your many different roles, traits, experiences and what you hope to achieve or the aspirations you have for your life.

Purpose is not just what you're doing, it's who you're being and what you're feeling as you go about your day. It gives direction to your values by providing an outlet for you to show them. For example, if your identity is 'I'm a maternal nurturer' your purpose might involve mentoring others, being a teacher or providing childcare.

When you are in the thick of burnout, it can be hard to figure out how you want to be or what you want to feel, let alone your purpose.

Using Your Values

There are several ways that you can explore the values you connect with, but it's as simple as a list you can download from my website at www.buffertheburnout.com.au. This is a list of words that demonstrate values that many people might identify with, but you can add your own.

Begin with an extensive list and start to highlight values that stand out to you. Once you've defined your list of values, you can assess what your days look like. I mentioned before, look at your bank account. Does that reflect the values that you hold, or is this part of an outdated value that you once had?

Take a look at your week. Pull out your calendar and see if the activities you're doing are aligned with your current values. For example, if health is a value, how many times do you get out for a walk or go to the gym? Spend your morning at Pilates?

What about travel? If travel is a value, how many times do you get out of your city or town to see new places and learn new things from other cultures? Is it only on special occasions, or do you take small trips over the course of the month, with bigger trips overseas or interstate?

When I first did this activity, I found it difficult because I knew what I didn't want. I didn't want to be spending time in back-to-back meetings with no room for creativity. But I just could not plan or envision what my day could look like without that.

It makes sense that I had such a hard time defining what was important to me because when we experience constant and chronic stress, the brain is sending signals that we are not safe. In the brain this function is performed by the amygdala, a little almond-shaped structure that is always on and scanning for safety. When it perceives danger, it sends the signal to the brain and body to go into survival mode and shuts down the ability for reasoning and logical thinking. It is known as the amygdala hijack to ensure we survive in the most efficient way. We move towards pleasure and away from pain as much as possible. Sometimes this means that the current state that is familiar to us seems like the better option compared with the extra time and energy it would take to make a change and do something new. You might stay in the daily grind because your brain is in this survival mode and shutting out other possibilities.

It's okay for values to change as we age or as seasons come and go, because different things happen in our lives over time. For me, children are an important part of my life. Being a mother was part of my identity for such a long time. But of course, the role of mother is to make yourself redundant. So, once I had made myself redundant, what was next for me? I was then pouring my mothering into creation as a manager of corporate services and opened a new school. Creativity is one of my core values, and it made sense that I would create a school from scratch.

Sometimes it's not necessarily that you're conflicted with your values. It may just be the season and time of life that you're in. If you're making an intentional decision and moving with purpose aligned to that season and that value, you will feel success, joy and fulfilment. It's when you are not clear on your values or living with a constant misalignment that you get the feeling that something is off.

BUILD YOUR BUFFERS

Assess your wheel of life

Complete the activity called the 'wheel of life'. There's an example in the appendix or download the full version from www.buffertheburnout.com.au. In all the different areas of your life, assess how satisfied you are in each of those areas on a scale of 1 to 10. Health, finances, intimate partner relationship, broader relationships and work are the most common, and you can edit to fit your own lifestyle.

The next step is to reflect on your ratings. What does that wheel of life tell you?

Does it make sense that the highest ones are where you've spent your time and energy? Wherever your attention goes, grows.

Are those areas aligned with your values, or maybe something's missing?

In this instance, choose the areas with the lowest scores and put some small action steps into place to start shifting the focus.

The good news is that you can align your goals to your values, or you can change your values to your goals.

Celebrate your 80th birthday
One of the ways you can identify your values is by using a method called the 80th birthday reflection. Transport yourself to the future and imagine it's your 80th birthday. You are celebrating surrounded by your loved ones. Family, friends, neighbours, people you've worked with share their fond memories of you and what you mean to them. They describe you as a person and what you stood for and what they love about you.

1. **Visualise the future**

    Get specific about where you were and who was there; for example, I am at home in a comfy lounge and surrounded by my children, grandchildren and great-grandchildren.

2. **Listen and observe**

    Now write down the specifics of what they say about you; for example, the grandchildren tell stories of how I was always there to watch them play cricket and make nourishing dinners to share with them every Sunday night.

3. Reflect
You can ask yourself, 'What would that person value in order for those words to be true?' What would that look like? How would you think and feel, and what would you do each day?

4. Act now
What is one action I could take now that would reflect that future vision? For example, if one of my values is family time, my calendar would be filled with time with my family. I would be able to stick to my commitments, be clear on my work times, leave work on time.

You literally could practise being that person today. You could practise it now. Log off your computer and go home.

This activity helps to clarify priorities in a broader sense and at the same time can inspire day-to-day action that is aligned with the vision. You will also very quickly see if there are misalignments in the way you currently live compared with your ideal values.

> If you are still stuck and looking for a guided version to identify values, download the list of values from my website and have a go at narrowing them down. Then ask the questions: Are these the values I want to live and breathe? Are they working for me? Where am I aligned, and where am I not?

CHAPTER NINE

LEVERAGE THE MIND

The mind is truly a fascinating part of being human, so complex we are learning more about it as we evolve. It can be likened to a supercomputer with intricate processes, both chemically and metaphysically. Every human has a unique experience of life based on their mindset and previous thoughts. What we think determines how we feel and subsequently how we behave, and 90% of what we think is repetitive.

Here's an example of how this played out for two team members I worked with. It's 10 a.m. and Kate and Jill are in a meeting with the leadership team discussing the progress of a current project. Their manager asks some clarifying questions about parts of Kate's and Jill's individual reports.

Kate provides her answers sheepishly and thinks she should have a more solid answer. Several people chime in with strong opinions on the report progress and Kate's shoulders slump as she starts to feel embarrassed and exposed. She feels the team thinks she is incompetent, feels attacked and that if she speaks up anymore, she will sound stupid. She starts thinking she is no good at her job at all and stops contributing to the conversation. She nods as others start to give their advice and leaves the meeting feeling depleted and isolated. During the rest of the day and into the night she replays the criticism and thinks about what she should have said and how she might call in sick tomorrow to save face.

When Jill is asked the same questions, she is momentarily flustered and doesn't have any answers but sits up and takes notes on the questions asked. She feels a little uncomfortable but thinks the feedback will be helpful to improve the parts of her work in the project. She asks more questions and engages in the discussion providing additional observations. As the meeting wraps up Jill proposes to follow up on the new ideas and leaves the meeting challenged but motivated by the work ahead. Afterwards she thinks constructively and plans how to investigate the improvements.

Same question but different experience for Kate and Jill. What is different in their thoughts, feelings and behaviours?

Kate's thoughts indicate she sees the criticism as a personal failure, whereas Jill sees the challenge as normal and an opportunity for growth. The questions from others for Kate provoke anxious and threatened feelings but for Jill, she feels more curious and open. Their behaviour plays out differently with Kate withdrawing and avoiding further participation whereas Jill becomes engaged with a solution-focused approach.

Through her research, psychologist Carol Dweck described these two experiences as a fixed mindset (Kate) and growth mindset (Jill). Those who show a growth mindset experience greater resilience during times of discomfort and tend to have the ability to view challenges as learning opportunities. Those with a fixed mindset, however, tend to experience more anxiety, worry and increased feelings of helplessness due to their belief that traits, such as intelligence, or skills like public speaking, are fixed from birth. Maybe you or someone you know has said, 'Oh, I'm just not good with numbers' or 'Writing is just not my thing'.

Whether we have a fixed or growth mindset is influenced by our early childhood experiences and how feedback and praise was given to us. As adults, how we respond to new experiences can be triggered from those subconscious thoughts and beliefs we've developed which then dictate our actions.

The Mind

The mind is more than just the brain, and our thoughts can be conscious or subconscious. Only 5% to 10% of thought is conscious. The conscious mind is the thinking mind that can reason and analyse. It is the part of the mind that our five senses deliver information to be interpreted. It is where discipline, so-called 'willpower' and choice exists. Any idea, thought, fact or opinion can be accepted or rejected by the conscious mind. If someone says to you, 'That dog over there is purple', and you're looking at the dog and you're like, 'Ummm, no. That's not purple, that's brown', it shows that your brain can categorise information by accepting or rejecting it based on what you already know.

Conscious thinking is accessed only from around the age of seven. Before that age, we are a human sponge, soaking in all the information and cues around us into our subconscious mind.

Ninety to 95% of our thoughts are subconscious.

We don't need to actively think about all the actions required to move our body to get out of bed, breathe or digest our food. Those things are automatic and driven by our subconscious. The subconscious mind also stores beliefs, memories and patterns of behaviours for our entire lives, and particularly those created in the first seven years of life before our conscious brain is online. During this time the subconscious mind can only accept ideas or thoughts and does not know the difference between real or imaginary thoughts. Everything that we see, hear, smell, touch, taste and experience forms our beliefs and is stored in our subconscious mind. The subconscious most often relates to pictures or images and is highly connected to emotions as lots of information can be processed quicker this way.

The subconscious mind is responsible for the moment you smell a vanilla cake, and you are transported to the times your mum baked one for your birthday as a child. You instantly feel the love and joy you felt at the time. Or perhaps that song you hear reminds you of the time your first love broke up with you by bringing back the sadness and ache in your body. These memories and emotional connections are stored in our subconscious mind.

It's the part of the brain that stores things that we're told about ourselves. Did you often hear the phrase that you are the funny one, or the one that keeps the family together? Or even comments you might have read from your teacher on your school report: 'Jane should focus more; she would get things done if she wouldn't talk as much.' These seemingly harmless (or helpful) comments can be hardwired into our brain, which is how our beliefs, our identity or how we see our place in the world are formed.

Repeat, Repeat, Repeat

Remember I said 90% of our thoughts are repetitive. Our brain looks for efficiencies and will commit activities to memory in the subconscious to be accessed later. You don't necessarily need to have a conscious thought to do something.

When I get out of bed, the first thing I do is brush my teeth. Then when I have a cup of tea, I open the kitchen blind. Those activities become what we call habits, and they become automatic when they are linked together with certain events and memories.

The body and the brain like to be the most efficient. It would prefer to use less energy to perform a task, and so what the brain does is put two actions together and wires them to make a neural pathway that is fast and efficient.

This is why it's automatic when we are skilled at something or used to doing certain things; it can happen quite automatically because we just repeat what we've done before. That one time you crossed the street, and a car almost bowled you over. Your body experiences a threat to your survival and the brain now has created an efficient neural pathway that reminds you to look both ways before you step out onto the road. The same process happened in Grade Four when you made a mistake in your class oral presentation and everyone laughed at you. You may have felt embarrassed and mocked by the group and your brain recorded this as unsafe so now you fear public speaking or speaking up. Some of our habits are helpful and some are not so helpful.

To make our brain even more efficient there is a part called the Reticular Activating System (RAS), which filters what we see in the world the way that we believe it to be. It means that much of how we see the world is according to all those internal beliefs that we've already established over many years as far back as early childhood.

The RAS acts as a filter for our conscious mind. The conscious mind is bombarded with billions of pieces of information and sensory inputs every day as well as over 60,000 thoughts that can overload the brain. The RAS filters the information to basically confirm what we already believe. Efficiency at its finest!

A common example of the RAS at work is when you decide, 'I want to buy a red sports car', and when you're driving to work the next day, all you can see are red sports cars everywhere. It's not that there are more red sports cars driving down the road. It's just that your RAS is now more *conscious* of the red sports cars that are in your field of vision.

Similarly, when you're feeling overwhelmed or stressed at work because your email inbox is overflowing, the RAS is going to continually filter what you see and confirm your belief that you're overwhelmed and stressed by finding more examples of where this is true. The physical piles of paperwork or the clutter that's forming in your wardrobe will become more obvious to you and perceived as more stress and overwhelm. Trust me, both these examples happened to me.

So, our thoughts and experiences create our feelings, which in turn create our actions or habits. Over time our actions and habits create how we see ourselves and our identity. The cycle continues with the mind and Reticular Activating System helping to maintain our sense of identity, whether positive or negative.

In burnout, we can feel trapped in a vicious cycle of overwhelming thoughts and negative patterns of behaviour that are self-perpetuating.

Rewire Limiting Beliefs in Five Steps

The good news is that you can use your thoughts to rewire your unhelpful beliefs, and you can use your actions to rewire unhelpful thoughts. It works both ways.

Let's go back to helping Kate deal with her stressful meeting where she felt attacked by questions about her project report.

Kate's limiting belief was that questions or feedback were criticisms and ultimately, she felt she had done something wrong. As we delved deeper, we discovered the belief was established in her early childhood experience of an authoritative dad, where questioning ('Why did you do that?') was followed up with her being 'in trouble'. This was reinforced when she was praised for being the smart one as a high achiever and the threat this praise would be taken away if she was wrong. Kate also remembered distinctly a time at school where a teacher asked a question and after she provided an answer, there were several kids who laughed at her. She never learned that questions could be curious in nature and were a way of collaborating with others. It meant that her body and mind were always on alert scanning for threats of criticism from others, leaving her feeling exhausted and alone.

To shift her mindset, we used Reframing to help her change the meaning of criticism she attached when people asked questions.

Step 1
Identify the belief. Ask the following questions:

- What did I believe in that moment? *They are attacking me.*
- What was the meaning I gave to their words? *They think I am not capable.*

Step 2
Challenge the belief. Now ask one or more of the following questions:

- What else could this mean? *Maybe they want to include more information.*
- What could be useful about this? *It might identify additional parts that I missed. It could improve the project.*
- What could be another perspective from your manager? *She is focused on getting the best outcome for the business.*

Step 3
Reframe a new belief. Write down an empowering belief. Use a notebook, sticky notes or even a whiteboard and place it where you can see it regularly. Use your fridge, your desk, your bathroom mirror or beside your bed.

- Old belief: *Criticism means I am a failure.*
- New belief*: Criticism is data, and I can choose how I use it.*

Step 4
Repeat the new belief statement each morning out loud. Use it before team meetings to anchor it in.

Step 5
Create a new emotional response.
Stand with your feet a little more than hip distance apart, hands on hips, elbows wide and head held high (like Superman; in fact, it is called the Superman Pose).
Practise saying out loud, *'Thank you for the questions. I don't have the answer right away but will get it before the next meeting.'*

Acknowledge, feel capable and celebrate when this happens in a real-life situation.

Combining the physical postures and saying the words out loud are critical to changing long-held beliefs. Don't just leave it in your thinking brain as you need to train your body and subconscious mind to believe it to be true.

Bonus Step Using the Reticular Activating System

Start collecting evidence of when you can accept the questions and feedback from others without the old patterns of negative thoughts. Your RAS will help you find examples and you can jot them down in a notebook. You might find there are examples of times that you used to overlook. Be specific in your examples.

- *When I entered the revenue data into the worksheets, Jane questioned why I used a negative figure for*

Tuesday. I explained to her it was due to refunds, and she was thankful for my accuracy. I felt calm giving the response because I trusted the data was right.
- *I created a draft of the team newsletter and asked Bridget for some feedback and edits. She gave me some ideas of what to change which helped improve the message for the part-timers. I felt proud that I could make it better for everyone.*

The Mindset Buffer

Burnout often results in you feeling helpless and stuck in a never-ending cycle of exhaustion and despair. Creating a growth mindset which views challenges as opportunities for learning creates a buffer that can shift that overwhelming feeling of stress every day. It helps to empower you by focusing on what you can control and that is, your response to any situation. This in turn helps break that cycle of hopelessness and gives you increased resilience and coping skills.

BUILD YOUR BUFFERS

1. **Do the five-step rewire process**
   Make changes to limiting beliefs and form new helpful beliefs.

2. **Collect proof of progress**
   Start a notebook to record evidence of when you notice how your old belief arises and when you behave according to your new belief as outlined in the bonus step.

CHAPTER TEN

RIDE THE WAVES

If I asked you right now to tell me how you're feeling or what emotion you are experiencing chances are if you're in burnout, you'd respond with 'I'm fine' or 'I'm good'. It's likely that lots of people ask you this, multiple times a day, but why is it that we respond with 'I'm fine' when really, we're not?

Fine is neither a feeling nor an emotion.

Fine is a socially accepted, automatic response we use at work or at the shops because we don't have the time, safety or space to fully go into how we are feeling. When we're in burnout we may not even know how we feel because in our busy day we don't have the energy or time to really check in. And sometimes it could be just a mask to others, or even ourselves, if something else much deeper we don't want to face is going on.

When you experience burnout, understanding the difference between emotions and feelings is important to interrupt the loop of what we call stress. We often think and talk about feelings and emotions as the same thing.

So, what is the difference between emotions and feelings?

Emotion is a physiological response to some sort of stimulus. Emotions are purely the chain of events that happens when the nervous system sends chemical messages to the brain and body signalling you are safe or not. They are automatic, universal and last for about 90 seconds.

The feelings are your thoughts, conscious or unconscious, that you use to interpret that emotion, so they come after the emotion. They can hang around for as long as you keep replaying the situation. Days, weeks, even years.

Let's start at the beginning with an explanation of the systems involved. It's complex but stick with me.

The Nervous System is your body's command centre that communicates endlessly what it needs to stay alive. It has two main parts:

- The Central Nervous System (CNS) made up of your brain and spinal cord. It receives information and processes it.

- The Peripheral Nervous System (PNS) made up of all the nerves branching out to your muscles, organs, limbs all the way to your five senses. It carries the messages between the body and brain.

Within the brain (CNS) is the limbic system with several structures that trigger your body's responses to make sure you stay alive. The main parts:

- The amygdala is your warning bell. Its job is to scan for danger. It's looking every day, every moment, scanning for any threats. Internal and external.
- The hippocampus stores and retrieves memories and stamps those memories with an imprint of the emotion that happened at the same time.
- The hypothalamus keeps your body in balance by triggering other systems to release hormones. It also acts as a bridge between the brain and the hormone messages from the Endocrine System.

The Endocrine System is made up of several glands that work by sending and receiving messages and then releasing hormones to trigger a response to keep that body of yours stable and safe. These are the main glands:

- The pituitary gland receives and interprets messages from the hypothalamus and sends further instructions to other glands.

- The pineal gland regulates sleep through the production of melatonin.
- Thyroid gland controls metabolism.
- Adrenals release the stress hormones adrenaline and cortisol.
- The pancreas is involved in regulating blood sugar.
- The ovaries and testes provide the reproductive hormones.

Now that you understand the systems and their purposes let's go back to the stimulus of an emotion.

The process starts when the amygdala notices a stimulus. Let's use an example of a loud noise behind you and the emotion of fear. Before you have time for conscious thought about what caused the noise your amygdala responds first. The hippocampus scans the memory banks to recall if this has happened before and if it is a threat. If yes, the amygdala sends an alert to the hypothalamus to tell the other systems the body is in danger.

The hypothalamus gets the message this is unsafe so sends a signal to the pituitary gland which then tells the adrenal glands to release hormones like adrenaline and cortisol. That's going to get you ready to fight or flee. All this happens fast, and your body will have physical changes like a rapid heartbeat, shallow and fast breathing, eyes and pupils will widen, and your muscles tighten.

Immediately you turn around and see a dog behind you who looks at you but turns and runs away. Now your nervous system will trigger a response and hormones to signal that you are safe. Nothing to see here. You might associate the feeling of surprise to that event and move on with your day.

Now, if the dog ran at you and bit you, resulting in pain and elevated fear because you couldn't get away until someone helped you, the feelings you associate to that moment will be much different. You start describing to the doctor as she patches you up that you felt helpless and terrified. You go home and tell your partner it was dreadful and relive the terror. You call your sister and tell it over again. You may even think about it as you lie in bed or the next day.

All the while your hippocampus stores the story and the emotion of fear with the feelings of being helpless and terrified. This could be triggered in future scenarios; whenever you hear a loud noise behind you, you experience the feeling of being terrified. Or it could happen by the sight of a dog. Your feelings keep the emotion alive, and your subconscious is responsible for over 90% of your feelings. That dog bite may have happened when you were three years old. You may not have a full memory of the event, but your body and brain will have stored it.

Emotion is a short physical wave. What keeps the emotions alive for longer periods is how we think, interpret and attach meaning, or worry about it happening again.

Emotions in Burnout

When you *think* you are feeling stressed all day, physically you may have been experiencing many short emotional surges over the day which you then have attached thoughts, memories and beliefs to tell a story of what that emotion means. Replaying the situations blends into one long and exhausting cycle of survival.

Here's how it played out for Kate at her brainstorming meeting when a colleague spoke over her.

- Kate felt the emotion of anger and her physical signs were increased heart rate, and tension in her shoulders, jaw and hips.
- Kate described the feelings of resentment, frustration and irritation. The feelings were shaped by:
    - **Thoughts**—*She disrespected me.*
    - **Memory**—*This is how my boss treated me last time and it ended badly.*
    - **Beliefs**—*My contribution is not valued, and I don't belong.*

Once Kate was more aware that the emotion and its physical symptoms would pass, she was able to catch them before they spiralled into the unhelpful thoughts and feelings.

Similarly, your thoughts and memories of feelings can stimulate the emotion attached to it. That's why when you hear a song that takes you back, you recall the joy of your high school dance. Maybe it's the smell of your mum's vanilla cake as an eight-year-old that you attribute to the feeling of pure love.

When we're in tune with our feelings and emotions, we feel much more connected to ourselves. When the body feels safe, we are better able to manage relationships and take care of the fundamental desire to belong.

Since emotions are physiological experiences, having a strong sense of regulated emotions also leads to better physical health. Without regulation, the constant cycle of high alert of being under threat can have lasting effects on things like cardiovascular health, etc.

Suppression Is Not Regulation

Self-regulation of emotions is a key skill in being emotionally intelligent. Once you're aware of the physical signals of emotions, you can pause and choose your response rather than react automatically. This is hard because the Autonomic Nervous System (ANS) produces responses automatically. As you've seen, the amygdala does this before you've even had a chance to think about it which is why it is often referred to as the amygdala hijack. It takes over before you know it and turns your prefrontal cortex (the thinking part of the brain) off. After all, when faced with a threat you just need to do the minimum to survive, not solve complex problems.

When we are in burnout, though, our entire day can feel like threats, but it would be a little unprofessional to get up and run from the boardroom table because you sensed a threat from a colleague if they looked at you with a steely gaze.

As a manager of a large secondary school, I had multiple responsibilities in a fast-paced, high-performing environment. I led several teams, and my work intersected with most people, up to 200 at one point. I moved through my day with back-to-back tasks, meetings, problem solving and care for my teams. I was good at self-regulation. Or so I thought.

What really happened was during the day I was experiencing a range of emotions, and feelings, but with no time to process them, I simply moved to the next task, meeting or activity. It got to the point where I wasn't even feeling or if I stopped to check, I could not name what I was feeling, except tired. Exhausted. Every day of the week. Then come Friday I would have a few glasses of wine to unwind, order takeaway food and flop on the couch in front of the TV. Some weekends I would doze on the couch for the whole weekend and do the bare minimum. For a long time, I thought I was tired and needed the rest, but I came to realise that the impact of chronic stress led to the activation of the dorsal vagal state in the ANS, otherwise known as freeze.

The Nervous System's Window of Tolerance

You now know the amygdala continuously scans for safety and then sends the signals to the body to change states according to the cues it receives. Polyvagal Theory explains how we move through these states using the Window of Tolerance.

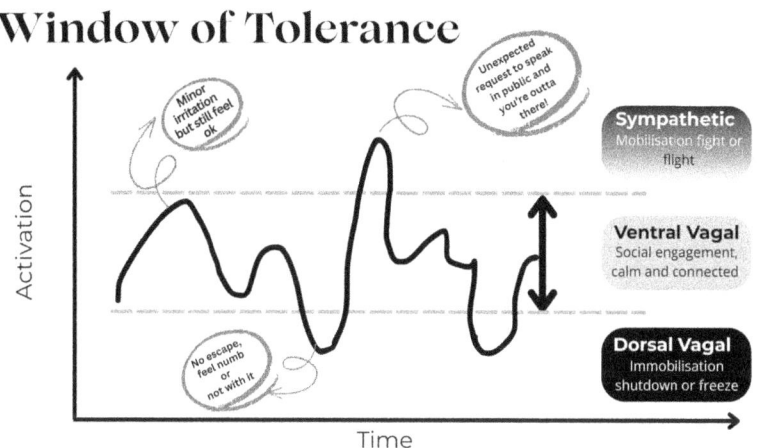

The body and brain attempt to keep us stable, and the default state, when it feels safe, is what is known as the ventral vagal state. We feel connected to those around us. Connection in groups provides a greater chance of survival than being on our own. It is the most beneficial state for our rest and digest processes to happen, for quality immune function and where we feel a sense of calm. This is your window of tolerance where you handle and respond to life with ease.

When safety is removed or the body senses a threat it sends a signal to ready the body for fight or flight. It is called the sympathetic nervous system and is triggered by the perception of threat or challenge. You might notice this type of state as a response to loud noises and any situations that are unpredictable or confronting. You might typically feel hyped up, restless, chaotic, angry or irritable. That high-alert feeling like you're ready for action.

When the perception of threat is so extreme and there's no possibility to either fight or flee, the most primitive response is the dorsal vagal state or freeze. You might have seen freeze in action when a kangaroo or deer runs across the road and instead of getting out of oncoming traffic it stops still and doesn't move. The freeze response is a complete shutdown of rational thinking, disassociation from the self and others, and somewhat running on autopilot. People often describe it as being numb, like you're there but not really there.

It's normal to move between these states and everyone has a different-sized window of tolerance. It's like a personal bandwidth for how you handle stressors. Your personal bandwidth can vary from day to day and at different times of your life depending on what you're going through. If you've had a sleepless night, poor food choices and you've got deadlines looming, your window might be narrower than last week.

In burnout the long-term triggering of the sympathetic and dorsal vagal states can lead to increased anxiety, outbursts of emotions, sleep disruption, poor digestion and suppression of the immune functions. Your window of tolerance can narrow meaning even small challenges can push you further into anxiety or shutdown easier and more often.

The good news is that you can use gentle, body-based somatic exercises to regulate the nervous system and expand your window of tolerance. They work through the body sending signals of safety to the brain engaging the ventral vagal state. Practices like breathwork from Chapter Two, gentle and soothing touch, grounding and using the senses to notice safety cues can signal to the amygdala that the environment and you are safe.

Regular activation of the ventral vagal state reduces heart rate and inflammation. This ultimately has an impact on reduced stress and illness over time, helping you recover from burnout.

Closing the Stress Loop

Emotions are not good or bad. They're just energy that moves through our bodies. When they don't move through, they can be 'stored' in the muscles and tissue of the areas of tension.

Robert Sapolsky, neuroscientist and primatologist, described the process of completing the stress response in his book *Why Zebras Don't Get Ulcers*. Sapolsky studied the behaviours and physiological responses of wild animals and compared them to the human. Put yourself into the life of a zebra and your biggest stress is staying alive. So, if a lion is chasing you, your goal is to get away fast. The physical response in the zebra is like ours. Release the stress response hormones to mobilise the body. Maybe the lion was tired and stopped the chase; the zebra will run a bit longer and once it's sure they've outrun the lion will return to their herd. You may observe them standing in groups under a tree and their bodies will shake and tremor to use up the remainder of the stress hormones produced but not utilised. Pretty quickly they will resume normal behaviour when their body systems have completed the stress response and returned to normal.

For you, this response happens when someone cuts in front of you in traffic or a car nearly runs you over. Same response physically and you get out of the way. The difference is that it is likely you retell the story to everyone you meet, replaying it in your head over and over. This thinking about it keeps the autonomic nervous system releasing the same hormones and stress response as it did in the real event. We can turn a single 'lion' into a week-long cortisol drip by thinking about it, talking about it, anticipating it and planning for the next time. It is this sustained release of stress hormone loops that increases our risk of illness and suffering. That in turn fuels the burnout.

BUILD YOUR BUFFERS

Meet and complete emotions and feelings.

1. **Ditch 'fine', use the emotions wheel to name it**
   Use any emotions wheel such as Robert Plutchik's or The Junto Institute's versions.
   1. Notice when you respond with 'I'm fine'. Or pause before you respond to 'How are you?'.
   2. Take a minute to scan your body for the physical symptoms. What is your heart, breathing, muscles doing?
   3. Pick a core emotion that is closest to what you are sensing. Choose from the six core emotions of joy, love, fear, anger, sadness and surprise.
   4. Move outward on the wheel to find a more specific feeling that fits. Example: core emotion = sadness / specific feeling might be disappointed.

Naming the emotion and the feelings that follow is the first step to breaking the loop that fuels burnout.

It short circuits the amygdala hijack and engages your conscious mind.

2. Be a zebra and complete the process
1. For anger and other hyper-related feelings down-regulate by screaming or punching into a pillow on your hands and knees. Use a pillow so the neighbours aren't alarmed but let the frustration and anger release.
2. Vigorous exercise like jumping or running is helpful here.
3. In a freeze or a dissociated response, up-regulate and reconnect with your body by placing your arms across the front of your body and squeeze down your arms and start to reconnect with the feeling and sensation of being you.
4. Look around and find five things that are red, listen out for four things you can hear, identify three things that you can touch, two things that you can smell and one thing that you can taste. This provides a lot of opportunity for you to reconnect with your body and your surroundings.
5. Walk outside and feel the cold breeze or maybe have a cold shower. You might also walk outside barefoot and just place your

> feet in the grass or the dirt. Put your hands on the dirt as well. This helps you reconnect your body and ground you.

CHAPTER ELEVEN

DO LESS, LIVE MORE

For someone who loves to experience life and everything the human journey has to offer, it's easy to end up with far-ranging interests over time. Add to that the many roles we take on. Roles like being a partner, a parent, a colleague, a volunteer, a carer of animals and on top of that, managing the basics of life like self-care, keeping a roof over your head, and feeding yourself and possibly others. We often make it so complex that it becomes overwhelming. In your desire to juggle all the things, you start looking for a better way. A better way to do more stuff in less time. Be more efficient and productive. You need better time management!

But here's the truth: you simply can't manage time.

Time is its own entity. You can't rewind it. You can't fast forward it. As much as I love the idea of Marty McFly jumping back and forward through decades in *Back to the Future*, or the endless repetition of *Groundhog Day* to get it right, the reality is we don't get do-overs. Time moves forward whether we like it or not. With or without us.

That's exactly how life felt for me when I was deep in burnout. Like a mouse on one of those little wheels, every day was on repeat, and for a long time I couldn't find the circuit breaker that would set me free and allow me to be more relaxed and do the things that mattered most.

The Myth of Time Management

We all know time is finite, but here's the kicker. None of us know exactly how much time we've got. That makes it even harder for the planners among us. How do you fit everything you want to do into a window of time you can't even measure?

I read everything I could about productivity. My logic was simple because if I had all these ideas and interests, surely if I could just do them more efficiently, I'd be able to do *everything*.

The truth is that's the fastest way to melt down your body and brain until you can't do *anything*, leading to even more burnout symptoms where your productivity is reduced.

The schools of thought around productivity are wide-ranging. Some say start your day with the hardest, ugliest, most dreaded task and your day can only get better from there. Others say start the day with quick, easy wins. They all work in their own way.

For example, quick wins spark dopamine, the brain's feel-good chemical, which helps you build momentum. But if you stay stuck only on the small wins, you might never get to the big, important stuff. Have you ever wanted to learn a new language and just never seem to get around to it?

When you have long lists of unfinished tasks or goals, you start identifying as a procrastinator. And procrastination isn't just avoiding the big things; sometimes people avoid the little essentials too, like eating, showering or responding to a simple text message.

If it's not simply about managing time, how do you get to do the things that are important to you?

Big Rocks

One of my favourite demonstrations of how prioritising the important things makes a difference is a story told of a professor's jar experiment I came across on YouTube by Stephen Covey. He brings out two jars along with big rocks, smaller rocks, sand and water. He asks students to fit the most items into the jar. Many begin with sand or small rocks, then add the big rocks on top. But the professor flips it and put in the big rocks first, then the smaller rocks fell in between the big ones, then the sand and water filled in the gaps around all the other rocks. He was able to fill his jar with more product than the students did by starting with the big rocks.

By starting with your 'big rocks', the things most important to you, you can fit the rest in around them.

I loved this concept. For years, I started my to-do lists by tackling the big rocks first. But when I was in burnout, I discovered I simply had *too many big rocks*. Instead of narrowing them down, I kept trying to squeeze more in.

Eventually, I decided that the concept didn't work for me. Insert facepalm emoji here.

Productivity had once been my superpower. I was known for getting things done at lightning pace. But I constantly underestimated how long things took, overloaded myself and ignored the red flags.

Despite doing so much, something was missing. There were big-ticket tasks that I never seemed to get around to. At the end of most days, I went home, despite having done so many tasks, feeling like a failure because I had missed another deadline or not started the big projects that inspired or energised me.

When I later asked family and friends to describe me when I was in the depths of burnout, they all said the same thing. *You always took on too much, want to do it all and don't do what you say you're going to do.* It was a hard pill to swallow. I justified this in my own head knowing that of course I couldn't do what I said I would do because I had too much to do! Red flag!

But they were right. Maybe I needed to do less.

Learning to Stop

When I was searching for the answer of how I could feel less shattered and exhausted, I did what normal people do and booked a holiday. Normally, my idea of a travel holiday was 'pack in as much sight-seeing as possible'. Six weeks through the US? Every city, every sight, every moment seeing and doing something fun and amazing.

But this time, we went to a small island in the Maldives. It wasn't small, it was a *tiny* island you could walk around in 25 minutes. Apart from swimming, snorkelling and a few water sports, there wasn't much else to do if you don't count eating and drinking.

And that terrified me.

I had booked seven days and started to panic. What if we got bored after we saw everything in a day? What if there was nothing left to see? I desperately wanted to rest, but maybe I had forgotten how to rest. Really rest with nowhere to be, nothing to do, no one to impress.

I had heart palpitations for the first two days.

But slowly, that eased. No internet. Sunrise swims. Sunset walks and talks with Geoff, my husband. Simple meals over the ocean. Quiet. By the end of that week, I realised, it was okay to stop. It was okay to do less. And it was one of the best holidays of my life. I make sure to book this type of holiday once a year now whether it be part of our big trip or small weekend getaways.

The Reality Check

Back at work, I wanted to hold on to that sense of calm rather than always rushing to get everything done. I decided to take a look at what takes up my time. On a Post-it Note, I scribbled a list of everything I did in just 90 minutes one morning. I ticked off 25 items. Some were small, like filed some notes from the day before, but many were big. Solving problems that required more than one step, supporting staff, strategic planning. No wonder I was exhausted. It was a lot.

Normally, I'd celebrate that level of output. Again, my superpower! But this time, I saw it differently: this is why I was drained. It was crystal clear to me that I *was* taking on too much.

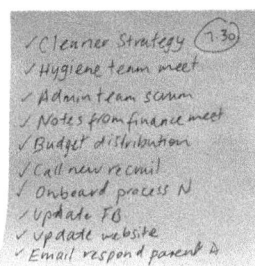 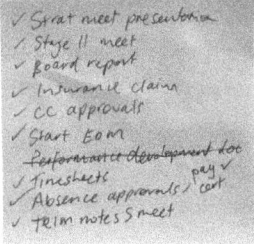 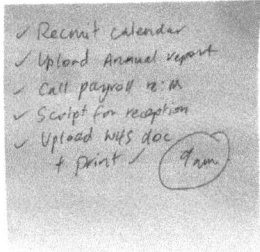

Decision Fatigue

At this point I knew I had to make some decisions about what my big rocks were and what I could leave out. But I couldn't decide. The chronic overwhelm in burnout also brings procrastination—aka decision fatigue. This is not just in your head, but a real phenomenon because having to make lots of choices requires a lot more effort for your brain. With so many choices and decisions every day, no wonder we shut down.

Take the example of getting a coffee. As a teenager getting a coffee simply meant a spoonful of instant stirred into hot water, or if you went out it was percolated and served with or without milk and sugar. Today? Ordering coffee can feel like sitting an exam. Do you want espresso, half cap, long black, flat white, latte, macchiato, mocha, cold brew, drip or nitro on tap? Should it be single origin, fair trade, organic, medium roast or dark? One shot or two? And that's before you even choose the type of milk or decide whether you want it hot, iced or blended. What used to be a quick pick-me-up has become a menu of dozens of decisions that leave you more drained and needing the coffee to pick you up.

That's just ordering coffee.

Add in all the other micro-decisions we make. What to wear, which way to drive to work, what to prioritise at work, how to juggle the budget, and by the time we get home, the thought of deciding what to make for dinner is unbearable. That's how food delivery apps use decision fatigue and the psychology behind it to market their service. Just sit on your couch and press a button and food will be delivered to your door. Phew! The decision is taken out of our hands.

How you handle decisions matters too.

In *The Paradox of Choice,* Schwartz discusses two distinct approaches people take when making choices. A maximizer wants the best, most effective choice. That means endless research, endless comparison and sometimes, never deciding at all. And when they do decide can often question and even regret the decision if they come across new information which would have helped in hindsight. A satisficer, on the other hand, simply chooses something 'good enough' that meets a set of acceptable criteria and moves on. The satisficer will prioritise speed and efficiency in decision-making.

If we go back to buying a coffee, a maximizer might get bogged down in looking at which coffee provides the most effective caffeine hit, carefully considering the ethical source or even going to great lengths to determine the biodegradability of the packaging. Oh, and then considers price!

Sometimes, you just need to be a satisficer. Choose any coffee and move on! Don't like it? Choose differently next time.

Doing Less, Living More

For me, the dopamine hit of ticking boxes was addictive. Productivity felt like proof of my worth. But when I learned to pare back, prioritise and eliminate unnecessary choices, I discovered a new sense of calm, more satisfaction and fulfilment.

Doing less allows me to give more to what matters—my health, my family, my freedom and creativity. These are the values I identified in Chapter Eight.

Empty Your Head

Reducing cognitive clutter means getting everything out of your head and onto paper or a digital list. One of the best techniques to do this is simply the brain dump. It's an easy task that can be done in as little as 20 minutes. Here's how.

1. Set a timer for 20 minutes.
2. Take out a clean sheet of paper (or a few) or open a digital note on your device.
3. Write down everything in your head.

I mean everything. Like a big, long to-do list. Don't freak out! You're not going to be doing all of this in the next days, weeks or even the next months, but it's a way of capturing all the information that you're storing in your head which is contributing to the decision fatigue, procrastination and overthinking.

Write down everything from the mundane to the big things in no particular order. Buy milk. Learn a language. Sell the old couch. Organise my photos. Call my mum. Organise my wardrobe. Let. It. All. Out. Be specific or be vague, it doesn't matter. If you find that you are really stuck, leave the note out on your kitchen bench over the weekend and just add things to the list as you go about your day. Need some more inspiration? Head to my website for some prompts.

Align to Your Values

Go back to Chapter Eight and review your values and the wheel of life. With this in mind, on your brain dump list cross off anything that is not aligned at this point in time. Here's an example. The very first time I did this exercise I had *Masters in Business Administration* on my brain dump list. Education is a high value of mine, but I was trying to simplify my life and didn't want to commit to several years of further education. I crossed it off the list and let it go.

You might have examples like *pay the electricity bill.* Take a highlighter or simply circle anything that is urgent and needs action in the coming week. Add these to your calendar or reminders on the specific day immediately. That will free up some worry and ensure you don't miss the urgent tasks.

Next take a different colour highlighter or put a box around anything that is a future action. If you had *birthday gift* which refers to getting your mum a gift, but her birthday is in two months, this would be a future action. Or you need to make a doctor's appointment for blood tests but there's no urgency to it. It could also include things like *learn a language.* Something you'd love to do someday.

Curate Your To-Do List

Now we want to reduce the decision fatigue to make it easier for you to choose to do the things you value without feeling the overwhelm of where to begin. It's likely you have lots of projects listed that require lots of smaller steps to achieve them. Things like *improve my health* and *organise my wardrobe.* Putting these on a traditional to-do list usually doesn't help you make decisions about what to do next. What often happens is you will scour your list for the easier tasks like *send email to Jane regarding budget.* Why? Because the simple act of defining the next, visible step makes it clear for your brain to recognise what to do.

When we constantly skip over that big project—*organise my wardrobe*—it's no wonder we feel like we are never doing what we *want* to do.

If I think about what the next step is to complete the task *organise my wardrobe* where would I begin? I might think that I need to repair those ripped jeans. Or there are the skirts that no longer fit on the top shelf and I need to donate them. But wait, I've got a basket of washing to do and I've found some odd socks without a match. It's at this point I give up because I don't where to start.

Instead of a general to-do list the concept of the next step, in *Getting Things Done* by David Allen, helps to reduce the decision fatigue by providing the next physical and small step to take in a project to move it forward. Each small step can lead to the next and so on until you complete the big task or project. So now my next three steps to organise my wardrobe might look like:

Take everything off the top shelf and sort into keep/donate piles.
Buy 10 matching coat hangers from Kmart.
Spend 15 minutes today folding T-shirts into the drawer.

The concept works for small projects and even larger projects at work. Sometimes the next step might be just thinking about how to go about the project or doing some research. In each case you can write the next step beginning with a verb. As my Grade Four teacher taught me, a doing word. If you need to think about a project like a workplace health presentation, the next step may be *brainstorm topics for workplace health.* Or if you want to learn a new language your next step might be *search for Italian teachers in the area.*

This simple hack to how you write your lists can help reduce procrastination and get you on your way to feeling like you're spending time on things that matter rather than lost in overwhelm. Add your next steps to your day planner or task list now. Aim for no more than three of these per day. You don't need more on your list, you need less.

Create Rituals Not Just Goals

Another way that we can reduce decision fatigue is by making tasks and activities that are important to us automatic. We refer to these automatic behaviours as habits. Habits are behaviours that we do as part of a routine. Bodybuilders have the habit of training regularly in the gym lifting weights and smokers might have the habit of having a cigarette after every meal.

Most people think that habits are either good or bad, but habits are just a response to either an external stimulus or our internal thoughts or feelings. Remember as humans one of our primary goals is to stay alive and do it in the most energy-efficient way? When we respond in a way that achieves that, our subconscious stores that information and will draw on that memory of safety to do the same behaviour again and again.

When I completed my wheel of life and identified that I really need to focus on improving my health I decided that I wanted to prioritise exercise and eating breakfast first thing in the morning. I knew that this would help me stabilise my hormones, improve my mood and support energy throughout the day so that I could make other positive decisions, like getting home from work on time.

My next step was to set the alarm for 6 a.m. and go to the gym, then eat breakfast before showering and heading off to work. What actually happened in the first few days was that when the alarm went off in the morning, I felt tired, and it was cold. I hit the snooze button several times until the point where I only had half an hour to get ready to leave for work. So, I dragged myself out of bed with no time for movement, let alone making a nutritious breakfast. *I'll do better tomorrow, I promised myself.*

What this gave me was a sense of comfort (by doing the same thing I did every day) and maybe a perception of extra rest. My habit loop was working perfectly, keeping me warm and comfy and maybe a few minutes of extra sleep. My brain was prioritising the most energy-efficient option instead of the extra effort required to change the behaviour to exercising and preparing breakfast. It felt like I was surviving and in the long term was just further sabotaging my health goals.

Creating habits that stick requires a bit of thought and preparation to eliminate decision fatigue by using the cues to prompt your brain into the desired action. I made it easier on myself by preparing a chia pudding the night before and had it ready to grab from the fridge. I put my workout clothes, sneakers and headphones beside my bed. Right where my feet drop as I get up. Instead of driving to the gym, I commit to just walking 15 minutes around the block, and I would listen to my favourite audiobook.

This time when the alarm went off the first thing I see is my workout gear. I slip them on, press play on the audiobook and head out the door. Before I know it, I'm home and head to the fridge for my breakfast. No need to cook or fuss. Just eat. I feel so accomplished having prioritised myself without feeling so overwhelmed by having to make the decisions early in the morning.

Over time I have been able to use the same technique to slowly and incrementally add to my morning routine to create a ritual. When we are looking to achieve longer-term goals, it's a long wait for the habits every day to get us to the outcome and reward. Routines can become a bit ho-hum and tedious. Creating rituals, however, can increase your feelings of satisfaction while you are doing them.

Habits are the tasks we do, and rituals are how we do them. Remember how Mary Poppins sugar-coated cleaning the nursery for the children by making it a game? Reframing the mundane activities into rituals that are enjoyable brings the reward into the activity itself. No longer is self-care just another task on your to-do list but rather a nourishing and enjoyable ritual to reduce overwhelm and prioritise you!

When Rachel, 49, came to me for help with her overwhelm, she told me she wakes up each morning with her mind racing. She checks her phone before even getting out of bed, scrolling emails, news headlines and reminders of all the things she should be doing—yoga, journalling, a healthy breakfast. It all feels overwhelming. With so many possible 'good' routines, she ends up doing none. By 9 a.m., she's already frazzled and behind, thinking, *I've failed again.*

When I worked with Rachel we stripped her morning routine down to the essentials. No perfect routine, no long checklist. Just three tiny steps:

1. Make a cup of tea with breakfast (prepared the night before).
2. Sit by the same window for five minutes of quiet.
3. Write one line about what matters most today.

It feels almost too simple. The ritual takes less than 10 minutes yet brings her a sense of calm and clarity. She notices that, unlike her old mornings filled with guilt and pressure, this ritual leaves her feeling quietly successful. Satisfaction comes not from doing *more*, but from doing the *right things in the easiest way possible.*

BUILD YOUR BUFFERS

1. **Empty your head**
   Do your brain dump. Get everything out of your head and onto paper.

2. **Curate your to-do list**
   Revisit your values and wheel of life from Chapter Eight and cross off items that don't align. Simplify choices by writing your next steps using a verb. Add up to three per day to your next actions list.

3. **Automate daily rituals**
   Reduce decision fatigue by preparing cues to stack habits and make mundane activities enjoyable and automatic.

CHAPTER TWELVE

GIVE YOURSELF A BREAK

Throughout this book I've reminded you that one of the brain and body's most important functions is survival and keeping you safe. When you're in burnout, the overwhelm and desperation you feel are signs of your body's protective mechanisms at work. And then you hear that little voice inside you saying you're not good enough. Your inner critic is simply shouting the loudest *You're not safe and doing this might leave you isolated.*

Sometimes all we need to do is listen to that inner critic and acknowledge the job it has been doing to keep us safe up until now. There's no need to try to get rid of it. That internal dialogue has its place. It can keep us safe, but it can also be very loud and overbearing when we might be served better by our caretaker or inner child voices. What we may need instead is to uncover the compassionate part of ourselves and get curious about the inner critic in a kind, friendly way.

Think about it. If a good friend arrived on your doorstep in shame, sadness, anger and despair, how would you respond? Would you berate her, tell her she should have known better, that she got herself into this mess, and she just needs to pull her big-girl panties up and do better?

Of course not. You'd invite her in, make her a cup of tea, put your arm around her and listen empathetically. You'd comfort her. Encourage her.

Self-compassion is the skill of turning that empathy inward and comforting ourselves the way we comfort others.

If your inner critic is telling you, *I can never meet deadlines,* meet that statement with curiosity. Ask yourself: *Is this 100% true, 100% of the time?* Reflect on the times you *have* met deadlines. Maybe this week you missed one, but perhaps that's one out of 10. No one can achieve perfection. And it's perfection that holds us back.

We all have different parts. The inner critic is just one, just as we also have a compassionate part, a generous part, a selfish part. We're generous when we help our children or friends, and selfish when we need to protect our own energy. Each part has its own voice, role and intention.

Most of the time, it's simply trying to keep us safe even if the way it does that no longer serves us.

These parts were formed over time, often through childhood and past experiences. Sometimes they've served us well. Take the example of a woman in her 40s labelled as a 'control freak' who micromanages every detail to make sure things are always going to plan. But she has become exhausted and resentful of having to always be the one to make things happen. Her hypervigilance has been her armour of protection. Growing up in an unpredictable household, her ability to control equalled safety. For decades that vigilance and smoothing things over has kept her safe and successful. Even admired and promoted for her 'exceptional' organisational skills. But now, as an adult, she doesn't always need this shadow part to keep working in the same way. It's not always useful when it is over-functioning and becomes an identity that brings shame and burnout.

Three Steps to Self-Compassion

In *Self-Compassion: The Proven Power of Being Kind to Yourself,* Kristin Neff outlines three components of self-compassion. They are awareness, common humanity and self-kindness.

Firstly, become aware and recognise that the inner critic developed as a kind of protector and its intention was to keep you safe from shame, failure or rejection in childhood. When you notice your inner critic, you might journal or say phrases such as, *I understand this part of me is trying to protect me, even if its methods are harsh. Thank you.* When it's shouting that you're a failure, you might respond with, *I hear the part of me that says I'm failing, but that's not all of me.* This shift from judgement to curiosity softens the critic's grip.

Remember that imperfection is universal and all humans experience it. Instead of, *I'm the only one who can't cope,* self-compassion reframes it as, *Everyone struggles sometimes. I'm not alone in this.* Sometimes it can help to reach out to a trusted friend and confide in them. Chances are they will tell you that sometimes that's how they feel too.

Finally, treat yourself as you would a close friend. Replace *You're useless* with *This is hard right now. You're doing your best, and it's okay to rest.* Make that cup of tea or snuggle up in your favourite cosy blanket and take a nap.

This creates a more balanced dialogue between your parts; rather than letting the inner critic dominate, you invite compassion, set healthier boundaries and allow space for kindness with yourself.

AFTERWORD

You will burn and you will burn out: you will be healed and come back again—Fyodor Dostoevsky.

Congratulations! You've reached the end of the book. Or maybe you just flipped to the back, hoping to find the shortcut you've been searching for to recover from burnout symptoms? Either way, you're in the right place.

But I hate to burst your bubble! Burnout is not simple, and there's no single way to recover or prevent it. It's as complex as we humans are. You've probably seen social media posts and influencers claiming they have a simple three-step method to fix your burnout and live an amazing life.

It's just not true. You're not broken because your body and brain is working exactly as it is meant to by keeping you alive in the most efficient way possible. Symptoms of burnout can't be fixed with a one-size-fits-all prescription. It is a journey of personal discovery.

When I started writing this book, I said you didn't need to follow each chapter in order, you could skip around depending on where you were starting from. For me, in my own burnout recovery journey, I did follow these steps sequentially and I have moved back and forth over the last couple of years to reset each focus as needed.

Focusing first on the tools in Parts One and Two to regulate my hormones, food, sleep and movement gave me a sense of control over a mind and body that felt like it was spiralling out of control. It helped my brain and body function better so I could reconnect with how I saw myself, my values and my purpose.

When I eventually did the activities around identifying values and working with the wheel of life (Part Three), I thought, *This is where burnout recovery starts.* If I had started at values, maybe my recovery would have been faster. There's that high-achieving perfectionist again! The truth is without doing the very basics to get my physical body in better health I could not identify my values or even envision what my life could be like. It took several attempts for me to get more connected to my values, but once I did, things became clearer. Journalling and writing them down gave me even more clarity.

AFTERWORD

Each chapter really does open the door to the next, and by the time I had clarity on my values, I began to use mindset tools to put more actions in place. That, in turn, deepened the connection between my mind and body and opened up my ability to feel again. I could recognise and ride the waves of emotions without attaching the automatic programming from childhood and created little rituals so I could rediscover joy.

There's no single magic pill or approach to help you recover and prevent the symptoms of burnout draining your energy; it requires your mind, body and spirit to work together. So start wherever feels right for you. Throughout the book I have provided stories and tools to help you build the buffers relevant to you. All the tools are underpinned by some science (because I am nerdy like that) like NLP (neuro-linguistic programming), Polyvagal Theory and CBT (Cognitive Behaviour Therapy). The magic happens when you take action and apply them. Consistently.

I have collated the tools into one easy reference here for you and do hope you use all or some of these to reset your body, rewire your mind, reclaim your spirit and *Buffer the Burnout*.

BUILD YOUR BUFFERS TOOLKIT

Page 31	4-7-8 Breathing
	Box Breathing
	Alternate Nostril Breathing
Page 47	Eat a variety of plant food
	Practise mindful eating
Page 61	Create your wind-down ritual
	Use calming affirmations
	Journal daily reflections
	Track your sleep patterns
Page 71	Add movement snacks
Page 85	Ask for edits
	List your tiny triumphs
	Build a boundary
Page 92	Make something with your hands
	Write something down on paper
	Read something new
Page 108	Assess your wheel of life
	Celebrate your 80th birthday
Page 125	Do the five-step rewire
	Collect proof of progress
Page 149	Ditch fine
	Be a zebra
Page 161	Empty your head
	Curate your to-do
	Automate daily rituals
Page 165	Give yourself a break

ABOUT THE AUTHOR

Nicole Cooper has spent more than 17 years leading and supporting teams across primary, secondary and distance education in Western Australia's public schools. A passionate advocate for lifelong learning, she brings her love of growth and curiosity into everything she does—helping others learn, lead and live with more balance and intention.

Her own journey through burnout became a powerful catalyst for change. What began as exhaustion and overachievement evolved into deep self-discovery, as Nicole learned to listen to her body, honour her emotions and rebuild her sense of self from the inside out. That experience sparked her mission to help others buffer against burnout and rediscover the joy of being fully human.

Blending neuroscience, somatics and lived wisdom, Nicole has a gift for translating complex frameworks into simple, practical steps that create real transformation. Her coaching and writing invite readers to think deeply, feel fully and approach growth with compassion rather than pressure.

With qualifications in Education Business Leadership, Fitness, The Mind School Method and professional coaching, Nicole combines evidence-based insight with heartfelt authenticity.

Fascinated by how the body works and the nervous system's quiet intelligence, Nicole finds calm in nature, perspective in movement, and joy in her family life as a mother of four grown children and *Mimi* to two lively toddlers.

Those who know her describe her as both inspiring and deeply human—a woman who has walked through burnout and come out the other side with wisdom, warmth and a renewed sense of purpose.

ACKNOWLEDGEMENTS
aka It Takes a Village

Writing a book has been a dream of mine for many years. As a young girl I would spend hours with pencil and paper writing pages and pages, even before I could form letters and words. I would draw little pictures for the covers and fold those pages to create my own books and use them to 'teach' my sister when we played schools.

This was one of the joyous childhood memories I had forgotten in all the hustle of adulting and so it has taken me 50 years to write my first book. I've learned in the last few years that reaching goals requires people in your corner either cheering you on, teaching you skills or guiding you to get there. I could not have written and published this book without the support, love, encouragement or teaching from many people, some of whom don't even realise the impact they've had.

First and foremost, my adorable husband, Geoff. The person who listens and indulges my most wildest ideas and lovingly keeps me going with fresh cups of tea, making dinner, cleaning the house. You show me your commitment to our growth every year when you hand over the organisation of our holidays entirely to me and then follow wherever I go. I'm so lucky.

Brandon, Cassidy, Katelyn and Jasmine, my origin story! Being your mother was everything I dreamed of and nothing I expected. You continue to teach me more about myself by reflecting what I need to see and I hope I was able to teach you a little something on the way.

My dearest friend Carolyn. You have been the inspiration for many parts of my life and cheer me on every step of the way. I love that our connection has spanned not just the distance but all of our eras. We continue to laugh, learn and grow closer every year.

Lucy, my mum, who modelled a fierce energy to life. The way you kept going through tough times gave me a resilience to strive for more. You are the example of how reinvention can happen at any stage of life.

ACKNOWLEDGEMENTS

Sharima, the younger, more attractive sister. I love the challenges of our philosophical, theological and sometimes wayward conversations.

Anita, my editor. Thank you for your patience and expertise. I've learned so much more about writing from the work you do.

Natasa Denman, the Ultimate 48 Hour Author founder and business guru. I am so glad I met you at that first seminar in Perth. Your go-getter energy scared the crap out of me and I just knew I had to lean into that. You are so generous in sharing your genius and such an inspirational woman. Thank you.

Melissa Hohaia, the lovely human who also happens to be a talented naturopath and women's wellness coach. The last three years working with you have transformed my body, mind and spirit. You've prescribed more than natural supplements and many of my lessons in here were born from our time together. I admire your brave and authentic teaching.

Breanna May for shining a light so that I could find my way out of the dark and shadowy places. You are an absolute genuine and genius woman and teacher! You reminded me of so much I already knew but had forgotten to trust. I want to be you when I grow up!

Courtney Wilder for challenging me. I was confronted by your bold, feminine, astrological woo-woo energy and you taught me to find and love that within myself.

Becks from Journey to Wellness. The somatic teachings from you were the game changer for my healing journey. You brought me the gift of a calmness I needed to connect back with my body.

Lauren Ohayan for restoring my core to help me rediscover the joy of movement and freeing me from the pain I felt in my body. The lessons I learned were a true awakening of my body-mind connection.

John Burke, the best boss, friend and giver of hope anyone can ask for. I learned to lead with compassion and care every day working with you. You believed in me even when I couldn't and held the space for me to cry and talk about menopausal symptoms whenever I needed to. Possibly all the time.

Gemma, my low-tox, holistic hairdresser and founder of Ardor Organics who specialises in beautiful, sensory healing experiences at the basin for women. You listened, provided counsel and cheered me on every step of the way.

Courtney of Monday Project Co. for helping me find joy in dressing every day and loving how I show up every day.

ACKNOWLEDGEMENTS

Stephanie White of Steph Spills Ink for capturing my essence in photographs. You set the stage to allow me to shine.

Heidi Swapp and Becky Higgins, two friends on the other side of the world, connected by the worldwide web. You created beautiful communities for women to explore creativity and document their stories. I can't express how following you from the early 90s inspired me and kept me going during the good times and the hard times. I'm so thankful for your generosity.

Meagan Muntz, Fiona Winfield and Carol Scott (deceased), the most empowering women who lifted me up. Thank you for the incredible work we did together.

APPENDIX

Wheel of life

Think about the 8 life categories below (edit the categories to fit your lifestyle if you need). Assess how you currently feel in each area and rate them from 1 - 10, 1 being extremely unfulfilled and 10 being outstanding. Either colour or mark your scores with an x.

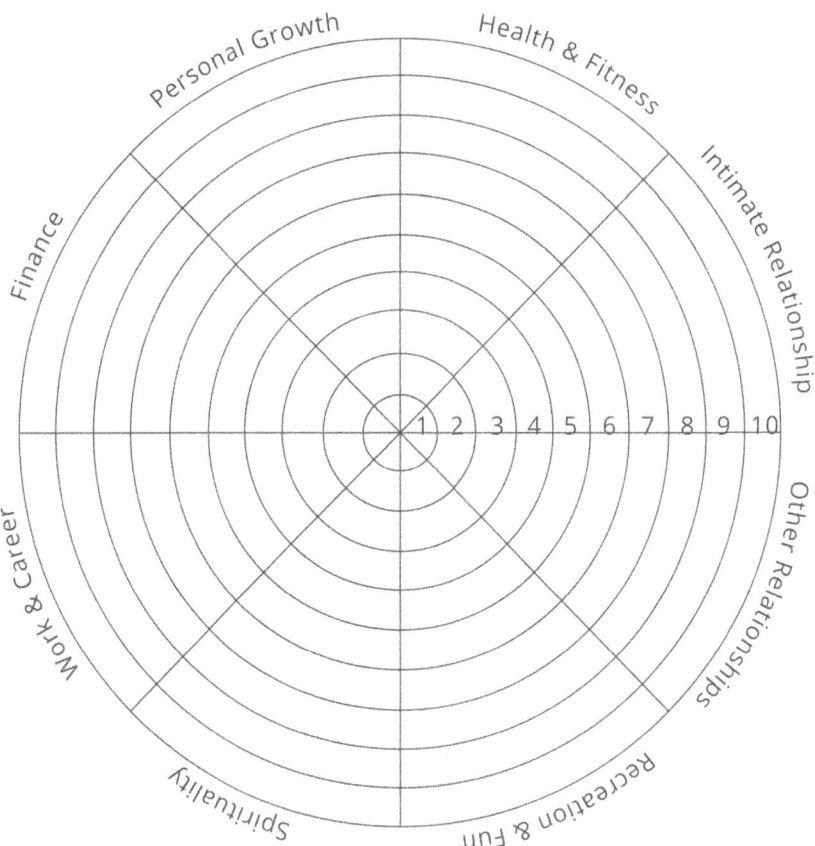

REFERENCES

My thirst for knowledge and love of learning means I read widely. There's so much to learn about the complexity of our human experience and what contributes to a quality life. I have provided this book as a guide for you to discover your own journey. The references here are what I found useful and combined influenced the topics covered in this book.

Allen, David. *Getting Things Done: the art of stress-free productivity*. Australia: Penguin Group (Australia), 2015 Revised.

Ballagh, Rebekah. *Soma & Soul: Somatic Practice Toolbox*. [Course materials] https://www.journeytowellness.online, 2023.

Ballagh, Rebekah. *Meet & Complete: Nervous System Guide*. [Course materials] https://www.journeytowellness.online, 2024.

Beale, Michael. *NLP Submodalities. The Building Blocks of Experience*. NLP-Techniques.org https://www.nlp-techniques.org/what-is-nlp/senses-submodalities/, 2025.

Berardi, PhD John et.al. *No, Food is NOT Fuel. And thankfully, you're not a Ferrari*. Online: Retrieved from https://www.precisionnutrition.com/food-is-not-fuel, 2025.

Bradberry, Travis. *The New Emotional Intelligence*. Retrieved from Audible. Brilliance Audio, 2025.

Cameron, Julia. *The Artist's Way*. Great Britain: Souvenir Press, 2020.

Cherry MSEd, Kendra. *Left Brain vs Right Brain Dominance*. Online: Retrieved from https://www.verywellmind.com/left-brain-vs-right-brain-2795005, 2025.

Clear, James. *Atomic Habits*. New York: Avery, 2018.

Csikszentmihalyi, Mihaly. *Flow: The Psychology of Optimal Experience*. Great Britain: Perennial, 2008.

DeCesaris, Dr. Laura. *How Different Exercises Affect Women's Hormones*. Online: Retrieved from https://www.rupahealth.com/post/exercise-affects-on-womens-hormones, 2023.

Dilts, Robert B. *A Brief History of Logical Levels*. Online: Retrieved from https://www.nlpu.com/Articles/LevelsSummary.htm, 2014.

Godman, Heidi. *Regular Exercise changes the brain to improve memory, thinking skills.* Online: Retrieved from https://www.health.harvard.edu/blog/regular-exercise-changes-brain-improve-memory-thinking-skills-201404097110, 2024.

Goleman, Daniel. *Emotional Intelligence: Why it can matter more than IQ*. London: Bloomsbury Publishing Plc, 1996.

Haver MD, Mary Claire. *The New Menopause*. New York: Rodale Books, 2024.

Hohaia, Melissa. *Lighten UP*. [Course materials] https://www.melissahohaia.com/lightenup_learnmore 2024.

Hoobyar, Tom et.al. *NLP: The Essential guide to Neuro-Linguistic Programming*. New York: HarperCollins 2013.

Leonard, Jayne. *How to build muscle with exercise*. Online: Retrieved from https://www.medicalnewstoday.com/articles/319151#articleHistory-mnt-3902468 2025.

REFERENCES

May, Breanna. *Level Up Your Life*. [Course materials] https://www.breannamay.com 2024.

McKeown, Greg. *Effortless.* Great Britain: Ebury Edge, 2025 Revised.

Moore, Catherine. *What is Eustress? A Look at the Psychology and Benefits*. Online: Positive Psychology Retrieved from https://positivepsychology.com/what-is-eustress/ 2019.

Nagoski, Emily and Amelia Nagoski. *Burnout: The Secret to Solving the Stress Cycle*. Retrieved from Audible. Penguin Audio, 2019.

Neff PhD, Kristin and Christopher Germer PhD. *Mindful Self-Compassion for Burnout: Tools to Help You Heal and Recharge When You're Wrung Out by Stress*. New York: The Guildford Press, 2024.

Pontzer, Herman. *Burn: The Misunderstood Science of Metabolism*. Retrieved from Audible. Penguin Audio, 2021.

Porges, Stephen W. *The Polyvagal Theory*. Great Britain: W W Norton & Company 2011.

Robbins, Mel. *The Let Them Theory*. Australia: Hay House Australia Publishing Pty Ltd, 2024.

Sapolsky, Robert M. *Why Zebras Don't Get Ulcers*. Australia: Henry Holt and Co, 2004 Revised.

Thau, Lauren et.al. *Anatomy, Central Nervous System*. National Library of Medicine: https://www.ncbi.nlm.nih.gov/books/NBK542179/, 2022.

Thompson, Holly. *WA Principals facing burnout as they struggle with playground violence, vicious parents*. Online: Retrieved from https://www.health.harvard.edu/blog/regular-exercise-changes-brain-improve-memory-thinking-skills-201404097110, 2023.

van der Kolk, Bessel. *The Body Keeps the Score: Mind, Brain and Body in the Transformation of Trauma*. Retrieved from Audible. Penguin Audio, 2019.

Weaver, Dr Libby. *The Invisible Load: A guide to overcoming stress and overwhelm*. New Zealand: Little Green Frog Publishing, 2019.

Webster, Bethany. *Discovering the Inner Mother: A Guide to Healing the Mother Wound and Claiming Your Personal Power.* Retrieved from Audible. Harper Audio, 2021.

World Health Organization. *Stress Definition.* Retrieved from https://www.who.int/news-room/questions-and-answers/item/stress, 2025.

World Health Organization. *Burnout Definition.* Retrieved from https://www.who.int/news/item/28-05-2019-burn-out-an-occupational-phenomenon-international-classification-of-diseases, 2025.

WANT TO LEARN MORE?

Here are three ways you can connect with me to help you on your own recovery journey.

Head to www.buffertheburnout.com.au now to download FREE resources to supplement the book. You can take the *Burnout Self-Assessment Quiz* as a starting point along with more resources to help you track symptoms, log your progress and find your values.

NICOLE COOPER

AUTHOR, SPEAKER
PERSONAL & LEADERSHIP COACH

Her audiences walk away thinking differently, feeling deeply and equipped with tools to buffer the burnout before it begins.

Nicole Cooper is a dynamic speaker, educator and author of Buffer the Burnout—on a mission to help people live a life on purpose.

With more than 17 years of leadership experience in public education, Nicole has seen firsthand how even the most capable professionals can become overwhelmed by the constant pull to perform. After navigating her own burnout, she transformed her recovery into purpose, coaching others to lead with emotional clarity and sustainable success.

Nicole's talks are where science meets storytelling. Drawing on her background in education, coaching, fitness and NLP, she has a gift for turning complex ideas into simple, practical steps to create real change.

Known for her warmth, humour and relatable presence, Nicole doesn't just motivate, she helps people shift from surviving to thriving.

When she's not speaking or coaching, Nicole can be found outdoors recharging in nature, fascinated by the wisdom of the human body and nervous system. A devoted mother of four grown children and *Mimi* to two lively toddlers, she embodies the balance she teaches—grounded, curious and joyfully human.

SPEAKING TOPICS

◆ **Heart over Head:** *How to Lead with emotion without losing your mind*
✨Flip the script on emotional intelligence and why it's your leadership superpower
✨Learn how emotions are data not drama, and why ignoring them leads to burnout
✨Walk away with 4 simple body-mind techniques to restore emotional balance

◆ **Perfectly stuck:** *Breaking up with Perfectionism*
✨Discover how to banish that inner-critic that holds you back
✨Learn 3 easy steps to swipe right on progress and reclaim your energy for the things you love
✨Take home your 4-week action plan and tracker to release the stress cycle

◆ **When values collide:** *Why good teams underperform*
✨Identify and map the unseen drivers of behaviour
✨Learn the 5 team dysfunctions and how to turn things around in times of conflict
✨Take home the Team Values Alignment Blueprint to start with your teams today

LET'S CONNECT

0419 041 449
nicole@buffertheburnout.com.au
WWW.BUFFERTHEBURNOUT.COM.AU

BUFFER THE BURNOUT: A 12-WEEK GUIDED RESET FOR THE MIDLIFE WOMAN

Do you feel like you're running on empty, holding everything together, yet secretly unravelling inside?

Have you forgotten what it feels like to wake up clear-headed, calm and excited about your day?

Are you tired of being the capable one, always strong for everyone else, while your own spark slowly fades?

Join me to kick-start your journey to reclaim your energy, reignite your purpose and remember who you are. An immersion designed for women in their 40s and 50s who are ready to ditch the hustle and restore balance.

Each week you'll step into a live, 60-minute call that blends nervous-system regulation, emotional intelligence, nutrition, movement and mindset tools—all anchored by your beautifully designed workbook and reflection journal.

This isn't just another 'self-help' course. It's a rewiring. A return to safety and softness with a loving hand to hold all the way.

By the end of 12 weeks, you'll feel …

- Calmly Energised—more grounded, focused and balanced
- Emotionally Clear—confident to navigate stress and emotions
- Aligned and Purposeful—living by what truly matters
- Lighter and More Free—no longer defining your worth by the length of your to-do list
- Resilient and Radiant—equipped with tools to buffer burnout for good

Your course includes:

- 12 x 60-minute live Zoom sessions with Nicole Cooper, blending science, somatic wisdom and story
- Comprehensive *Buffer the Burnout* workbook and reflection journal to map your personal journey

- Weekly rituals and micro-practices to anchor calm and clarity in your daily life
- Gentle accountability and community with a circle of women who understand what it's like to carry the mental load and are ready to release it

Head to www.buffertheburnout.com.au to join now!

TESTIMONIALS

Nicole is an absolute inspiration. She has walked the talk and continues to be a dedicated evolver—knowing that you are never done growing as a human.

When Nicole first reached out for my support almost three years ago, she was pushing hard and blindly in the depths of burnout. She was sacrificing her health for achievements and gauging her success on the approval she received from others—which never felt like enough for her and left her bending over backwards to please. Her transformation from burnout and disconnection to awareness and embodiment is proof that anyone can pivot and claim a life they feel truly proud of.

Nicole has experienced first-hand the benefits of tapping into the wisdom of your body and the power of releasing yourself from needing validation from others. Being able to feel deeper into her emotions (not run away from them) and be guided (and motivated) by what her heart and soul truly desires is what has led her to where she is now.

Nicole has embraced the discomfort that comes when we truly choose to grow. She has been willing to face the depths of herself that were previously jammed down and kept tightly locked away. Her reward from this is a deeper sense of self and connection to the powerful woman she is.

She is aware that the journey is not over. I know that Nicole has learnt to lean into the parts that feel the most challenging and uncomfortable—because that is where the treasure lies.

It has been an absolute pleasure to witness Nicole claim herself.

Melissa Hohaia,
Women's Wellness Naturopath and Coach

As a coach and mentor, Nicole is so naturally calm and reassuring. It was great to have a trusting and constructive conversation with her about some of the challenges we face as a new school, and around our upcoming Compliance Review. It was great to check in with someone who understands my role, to give me feedback about what I could improve on in a positive way, and what I am doing well.

After my meeting with her, I had a clear action plan in place to prepare for our Compliance Review.

**Sian Keys,
MCS Burns Beach Primary School.**

I would like to extend our heartfelt thanks to you Nicole for stepping in at such short notice and speaking at our Forum Day event. Your willingness to share your personal journey through education, along with insights into your exciting new ventures, writing a book and producing a podcast, was both inspiring and uplifting. The authenticity and warmth of your presentation resonated deeply with our members, and we are incredibly grateful for your generosity in contributing to the day with such poise and professionalism.

Your ability to step up seamlessly, with short notice, was truly remarkable. It is not lost on us how rare it is to have someone who can adapt so effortlessly and still deliver such a meaningful and engaging session.

**Suzanne Rowley,
President,
WA School Business Professionals Association**

NOTES

www.ingramcontent.com/pod-product-compliance
Lightning Source LLC
Chambersburg PA
CBHW061218070526
44584CB00029B/3884